Creative 35mm Techniques

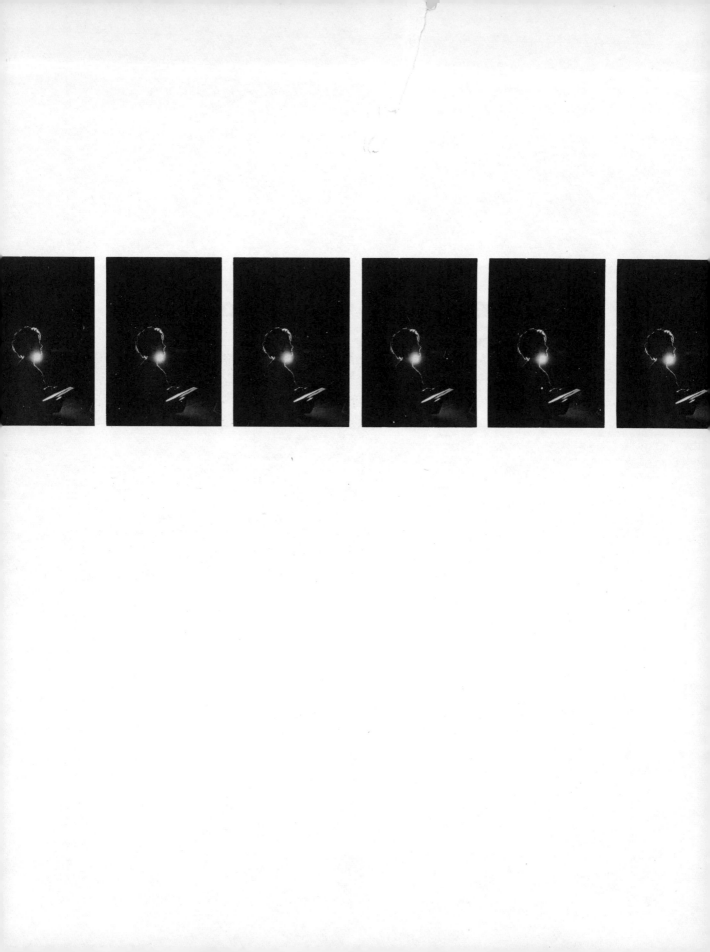

A. E. WOOLLEY

Creative 35mm Techniques

NEW YORK: A. S. BARNES AND COMPANY, INC.
LONDON AND TORONTO: THOMAS YOSELOFF LTD.

A ZIFF-DAVIS BOOK

A. S. Barnes and Company, Inc.
8 East 36th Street
New York 16, New York

Thomas Yoseloff Ltd.
18 Charing Cross Road
London W.C. 2, England

Printed in the United States of America

First printing June 1963
Second printing August 1964

9909

DEDICATION

In this book I would wish that words and pictures could be placed together so strongly that readers would be motivated to march as an army into the exciting unknown worlds that remain for photography and photographers. But the march cannot be to the cadence of old clichés and ideas. There must be thoughts that will lead to new thoughts. And new thinking, even if no ono agrees, must activate the chemicals of creativity to explore photography in yet unexplored territories. I hope that this book will set the tempo to the ring of new cadence. No army is any stronger or more meaningful than the individuals who compose that army. It is the individual to whom I offer my thoughts and techniques. If you enlist, my call to service has been answered. My companion, my fellow camera bearer, to you I dedicate this book.

PREFACE

In recent years two men of letters have been acclaimed by their peers as "great," "outstanding," and "creative." Both D.H. Lawrence and Henry Miller were being recognized for novels they had written twenty years earlier. And both novels were being singled out for their four-letter word vocabulary which had been the reason the books created international controversy. Yet through changing values, or reduced restrictions, both *Lady Chatterley's Lover* and *Tropic of Cancer* were printed in their entirety. And in the opinions of collective critics a new and important precedent had been established regarding vulgarity and creativity.

As a photographic writer I do not have any place for the four-letter words of Lawrence and Miller. Yet, there are four-letter words relative to the photographic process that I do have use for, and their application can create visually exciting pictures. Our four-letter word vocabulary consists of "film," "lens," "soup" (as applied to developer), "hypo," and "lite." These words make up the entire gamut of the photographic medium. Only the camera is missing. And since the camera cannot function without our four-letter words, perhaps it is reasonable to assume that no camera is an entity. To create pictures through the photographic processes, the photographer must know his camera—using it as a third hand, or using it with unconscious preciseness. And by adapting the four-letter words of photography to the many techniques of the camera, the photographer will reap the fullest advantages from the system of photography with which he has chosen to work. The 35mm system of photography is a photographic world of its own. There are mechanical means due to equipment available which extend the creative curve of the photographer. There are techniques that apply to all formats of photography, but which apply more readily to the 35mm school. Some of these techniques are the hyperfocal distance, depth of field, panning, selective focus, and the many lenses and devices over the lenses which alter the image.

The 35mm is not just the size of a camera. It is a way of life for the photographers who use and understand the medium. The crisp, minutely detailed picture, that long has been associated with the view camera is also possible with the 35mm format. The small camera is not the sign of a lazy or lackadaisical photographer. To the contrary, the 35mm user is a much more accomplished technician who is capable of producing the fineness of image that is the envy of the big camera user. The 35mm photographer has traveled from the age of Edward Weston to the age of W. Eugene Smith and continues to record our image of the 20th century, serving the role of historical and social documentation. From the serene scene of a first frost, to the conflicts of warring cannon, the 35mm techniques of photography have contributed, and will continue to contribute, to the images that reveal our world and our wonders.

The purpose of this book will be to stimulate the reader through words and pictures, to broaden his knowledge, and to offer techniques which might be new, or seldom used, yet creative, tools that can improve the photographs of 35mm photographers.

I do not intend to make this an "experience" book. But, because this book was conceived in the spirit in which I work, all of the information will be drawn from practical, workable procedures that I employ every day in my 35mm photography. And since I use the 35mm exclusively, this book will be my total approach to creativity through the camera.

A. E. Woolley

ACKNOWLEDGEMENTS

IN AN UNDERTAKING SUCH AS THIS BOOK, there are always contributors who cannot be thanked adequately. There are people who claim unsung credit: Dorothy for critical comments and the labor of editing, Ben Karp for "thoughts," Tommy Johns for the "how-to" holding of the camera pictures, and friends for encouragement. For the use of pictures I want to express gratitude to publications and people who have given me material rewards for the photographs I create: Betty Leavitt, *Look*; Ruth Block, *New York Times Magazine*; Howard Cohn, *Pageant*; Lee Hall, *Life*; Don Margargee, Central Hudson Company; Don MacIsaac, Ulster County Savings Bank; and the Cormac Chemical Company. For technical assistance I would like to thank Ken Poli, *Leica*; and Len Silverman, Nikon.

CONTENTS

Creative 35mm Techniques

PART I

The Camera

After pondering the problem, hearing more "againsts" than "fors," Dr. Leitz said, "We will produce the camera." And with his affirmative answer the *Leica* camera became more than an experimental object of curiosity. For the 35mm system of photography was born in the conception of the *Leica* camera. From that historic day in 1924, the thirty-five millimeter camera has progressed to the height never enjoyed by any camera or format and design. There are many competitors and imitators in the 35mm camera field and all of them make a contribution to the perpetuation of the popularity of the 35mm camera. But with the hundreds of cameras in the 35mm field crowding the camera store shelves, there remains only one major departure from the original Barnack design. There is the single lens reflex and/or prism reflex addition to the original rangefinder eyelevel type. Actually the first 35mm camera did not have a rangefinder, but the feature was quickly added to the succeeding model.

With 35mm cameras being made in Germany, Japan, the United States, Russia, and many other countries, there is a near saturation of supply and demand. There is a thirty-five millimeter camera to fit every pocketbook and every kind of photographer. To list and discuss all of them would take ten times the total space occupied by the contents of this book. Therefore, I have made only a partial listing of available cameras. But, for the reader's information there are good thirty-five millimeter cameras priced from thirty dollars to several hundred dollars. The quality of the lens, the shutter, and other gadgets, determines the price and longevity of the camera.

Since all thirty-five millimeter cameras fall in one of two major designs, my concern with the discussion of the camera will be with the importance of the design and

1. Adlai Stevenson, a portrait. The three elements of the composition of this picture were brought together with a 200mm telephoto lens. Mr. Stevenson, the silhouette of Roosevelt, and the "WE" were combined by the techniques possible with long-length lenses. (Taken for *Life* magazine.)

fluence over competitors and imitators. But not all of the eyelevel cameras of the rangefinder design are mere offspring of the *Leica*. The *Contax*, which was produced by Zeiss a year after the first *Leica*, contained many features that proclaimed it to be an original design. Between these two cameras which established and set the pace for all 35mm eyelevel rangefinder designs, all features of 35mm cameras may be found. Only the *Minolta*, with its interchangeable film back, has an entirely new feature. The *Robot* with its spring-driven multi-exposure technique was also new. Some of the 35mm cameramakers devised attachments to gear their cameras for multi-exposure shooting. Over the years the accessories and gadgets available for the eyelevel rangefinder cameras made it possible to have "many cameras in one," through the use of the extra attachments.

The other design that completes the pair of major camera types is the single-lens or prism-reflex type. With this camera, the picture composition is seen through the

its contribution to the creative act of making a photograph. Some of the equipment listed in this chapter illustrates the variety and price range of the hundreds of variations of the two principal designs; the rangefinder eyelevel type, and the single-lens and prism-reflex type.

The largest number of cameras are manufactured in the eyelevel and rangefinder design. Being the original design of the 35mm camera industry, the eyelevel concept of seeing has commanded great in-

2. The Leica system of 35mm photography forced the photographic world to develop a new concept of imagery and thought. The M-2 model shown here is the first major departure from the original Leica design of 1924.

3. The Leica reflex housing for eye level shooting with this rangefinder camera offers single-lens vision with the added versatility of a multitude of lenses.

4. The single-lens reflex Nikon is the first camera to convert the qualities of the range-finder camera to a true reflex single lens design.

same lens that will record the scene. Through the principle of a mirror reflecting the image, the subject is viewed on a focusing glass. The mirror drops out of view as the shutter is released to expose the picture. The *Exakta* pioneered this design and for many years was the only 35mm camera marketed with this design. From 1950 to 1960 the single-lens reflex began a ten year growth that is still climb-

ing. By the improved design of automatic diaphragms and improved camera mechanics, the single-lens reflex became an excitingly popular technique of 35mm photography. So strong was the technique felt in the industry, that the major eye-level camera manufacturers designed reflex housings for their cameras, or produced all new single-lens reflex cameras. *Leica* designed a prism-type reflex housing that fits the standard rangefinder camera and converts it to a single-lens reflex. Now, the newly designed Leicaflex is a single-lens reflex camera utilizing all of the Leica features and quality. Both *Canon* and *Nikon* produced all single-lens reflex cameras. The *Pentax* scored a hit with a finely produced camera in a price range considerably beneath the *Leica, Canon,* and *Nikon cameras.*

But with all the many cameras available,

5. A bellows and reflex housing converts the rangefinder Leica into a single-lens reflex camera with a working range from ultra-closeup to infinity, depending on the lens in use. Accessories like this extend the creative range of the photographer by making his equipment more versatile.

6. A 400mm telephoto lens was used to select these two kids out of a group of a dozen or more playing together. Their isolation is accentuated by placement and space.

and with all of the accessories to improve upon the cameras, there remain only two principal designs. Our concern will be with the designs and not the individual cameras.

The rangefinder camera has one very distinct advantage that offers a way of work which allows freedom from the camera mechanics at the time of exposure. The fact that the lens and shutter may be set, and no adjustment made at the time of exposure, is the feature to which I refer. Because you do not see through the lens which will take the picture, there is no need to set or pre-set the lens opening as with the improved automatic diaphragms

of single-lens cameras. The viewing and focusing of the rangefinder camera is separate from the lens which will take the picture. There is never any lost motion which might result in a missed picture. And there is always full vision of the subject and never a "blind" moment as results with most reflex cameras.

While there are disadvantages in using the through the lens design camera, there are very definite and distinctive advantages. The foremost advantage of the single-lens reflex, and especially with the prism finder for eyelevel shooting, is the chance to study the effect of optical control with a subject. With the single-lens you can see the effect of stopping the lens down for depth, or leaving the lens open for selective focus. You can pinpoint the focus to the exact spot desired. Without variation, the image seen on the focusing glass is the image that will burn invisibly on the light-sensitive film emulsion. Composition and use of total format are far more easily accomplished. The cost of single-lens reflex lenses is considerably less because the lens does not have to be fitted to a cam-focus lever. The single-lens reflex permits a barrel focus independent of the camera. The image is seen sharp on the focus glass.

But the single-lens reflex has two drawbacks. It is unusually difficult to work with unless a prism eye level finder is used to bring the focus surface closer to the eye. If you use the reflex without the prism, you still must bring the camera up to your eye for fine focusing. The very small image on the ground glass is entirely too small for critical study and focus of the subject. However, the prism-finder corrects most of this unworkable situation. Perhaps the most bothersome characteristic of the single-lens, and one which interferes with concentration of the mind toward creating pictures, is the "mirror-to-blindness-to return of mirror action of exposure." Even with the automatic diaphragms of the

7. Fine linear imagery is possible with the highly critical resolving power of the lenses of 35mm cameras. Even the inexpensive cameras will usually have lenses capable of recording sharp pictures.

8. Ilya Bolotowsky, artist. The use of a 125mm Hektar with the Leica Visaflex II made possible the isolation of the face of the artist within a geometric design, suggesting a similarity to his painting techniques.

newer reflexes, there is still a lag of time from exposure to the return of the mirror that momentarily leaves the photographer blind to his subject. The Pentax and several other cameras have eliminated most of the undesirable lag with a "flip-mirror." Both of these systems work on the blinking-of-the-eye theory. The mirror is returned to position in not much more than the wink or blink of an eye. Yet it is still a motion that could and does interfere with concentration toward the subject which is being photographed.

There is no way that any person can tell another which camera to use. For just as one car drives better for one individual, or a certain weight bat feels better to one baseball player, or one ski construction is preferred over another, there is a personal preference in the design and operation of a camera that determines the preference of one camera over another for the individual. The only way to discover your preference is to try cameras in each of the two basic designs and select the one that causes the least concern in operating it. The camera must allow the photographer to function with intuitive and instinctive ease. Otherwise, the instrument is a barrier which looms large between your creative instincts and the instrument of recording.

35MM CAMERA LISTING:

Under $100 rangefinder type:	Flash	Focus	Interchangeable lens
Aires Viscount 1.9	XFM	RF	No
Ansco Super Menar f:2.8	XFM	RF	No
Argus C-3 f:3.5	X	RF	Yes
Baldessa I f:2.8	X	Scale	No
Baldessa Ia f:2.8	XM	RF	No
Baldessa Ib f:2.8	XM	RF	No
Baldessamat f:2.8	XM	RF	No
Fujica 35-ML f:2.8	XM	RF	No
Graflex Century 35 f:28	XFM	RF	No
Graflex Graphic 35 f:2.8	XFM	RF	No
Koday Pony IV f:3.5	X	Scale	No
Kodak Signet 50 f:2.8	X	Scale	No
Konica IIIa f:2	XFM	RF	No
Minolta A f:3.5	XM	RF	No
Minolta V2 f:2	XM	RF	No
Olympus Ace f.2.8	XFM	RF	Yes
Petri Color Super f:1.9	XFM	RF	No
Ricoh 500 f:2.8	XM	RF	No
Robin LM f:1.9	XM	RF	No
Tower 18 w/meter f:1.8	XM	RF	No
Voigtlander Vitomatic I f:2.8	XM	Scale	No
Walz Envoy M-35 f:1.9	XM	RF	No
Welti f:2.8	XM	Scale	No
Yashica YL1 f:1.9	XM	RF	No
Contina-Matic II f:2.8	XM	Scale	No
Ikonette f:3.5	X	Scale	No

Over $100 and under $200:			
Agfa Ambi-silette f:2.8	XM	RF	Yes
Canon P f:2.8	XMFP	RF	Yes
Fujica SE f:1.9	XM	RF	No
Graflex Graphic 35NE f:2	XM	RF	No
Honor 35 f:1.9	FP	RF	Yes
Kodak Retina IIIs f:1.9	XFM	RF	Yes

Kodak Signet 80 f:2.8	XM	RF	Yes
Konica IIIm f:1.8	XFM	RF	No
Leica Ig f:3.5	XMFP	Scale	Yes
Minolta Super A f:2	XM	RF	No
Robot Star II f:1.9	XM	Scale	Yes
Tanack IVs f:2	XMFP	RF	Yes
Tower 45 f:2	FP	RF	Yes
Vitomatic II f:2.8	XFM	RF	No
Yashica YF f:1.8	XFP	RF	Yes

Over $200:

Canon P f:1.2	XM FP	RF	Yes
Canon VI-T f:1.2	XM FP	RF	Yes
Contax IIIa f:1.5	XM FP	RF	Yes
Graflex Graphic 35 Electric f:1.9	XM	RF	Comb.
Leica IIIg f:1.5	XM FP	RF	Yes
Leica M-2, M-3 f:1.5	XM FP	RF	Yes
Nikon S-3 f:1.4	XMFP	RF	Yes
Nikon SP f:1.1	XMFP	RF	Yes
Robot Royal f:1.9	XM	RF	Yes
Widelux FI f:2.8			No

SINGLE LENS REFLEX:

Under $100:

	Finder	Diaphram	Flash	In.ch. lens
Agflex f:2.8	WL	Auto	XM	No
Astraflex 1000 f:2.8	WL,PP	Man./Auto.	XM FP	Yes
Exa f:2.9	WL,PP	Man./Auto.	XM	Yes
Exa Automatic f:3.5	PP	Auto	XM	Yes
Miranda S f:2.8	WL,PP	Man./Auto.	X FP	Yes

Over $100 and under $200:

Agfaflex II, IV, V f:2	PP	Auto	XM	Yes
Auto Astraflex f:1.8	PP	Auto	XM FP	Yes
Contaflex f:2.8	PP	Auto	XFM	Yes
Edixa Reflex B f:2.8	WL,PP	Auto	XM FP	Yes
Heiland Pentax f:2.8	PP	Auto	XM	Yes
Kodak Retina Reflex f: 2.8	PP	Auto	XFM	Yes
Miranda D f:2.8	PP	Man./Auto	X FP	Yes
Petri Penta f:2	PP	Man.	X FP	Yes
Tower 34 f:1.9	PP	Auto	XM	Yes

Over $200:

Alpa 4b f:2.8	WL	Man./Auto	XM FP	Yes
Alpa 5b, 6b, 8b f:2.8	PP	Man./Auto	XM FP	Yes
Besler Topcon f:1.8	PP	Auto	X FP	Yes
Exakta f:2	PP	Auto	XFM	Yes
Konicaflex f:1.4	PP	Auto	XM	Yes
Minolta SR2 f:1.8	PP	Auto	X FP	Yes
Miranda Automex f:1.9	PP	Auto	X FP	Yes
Nikon F f:2	PP	Auto	XM	Yes
Voigtlander Bessamatic f:2.8	PP	Auto	XM	Yes
Canonflex f:1.8	PP	Auto	XM FP	Yes

Code: RF-rangefinder
     X-zero delay flash
     F-gas filled bulbs 5 millisecond delay
     M-20 millisecond delay wire filled bulbs

FP-focal plane bulbs
WL-waist level finder
PP-pentaprism finder
Auto-automatic
Man.-manual

SEEING, ITS MEANING

Every time I have bought or obtained a new piece of equipment, I have been motivated to put the newly acquired item to immediate use. And with each new camera, lens, or whatever the piece of equipment, I have gained increased interest in all of my equipment. The use or application of the new item generally opens up new or exciting avenues that are oneway streets to new images. A new f:1.5 lens may allow the exploration of available light situations that the f:2 would not permit. A film speed of ASA 400 might permit pictures that were impossible with the f:2 lens. The photographer can broaden his scope of creativity and production of pictures by the acquisition of a new lens which is a new vehicle for seeing. Also, a camera of a different design, such as a single-lens reflex, will raise the curtain of creativity on a stage of imagery not possible with the rangefinder design. Telephoto or other length lens can contribute to composition that the normal lens disallows because of its fixed focus range and angle of vision. A new accessory can be the stimulation or motivation to pick up your camera and *look about*. The new gadget could be the factor instrumental in the production of a picture with a new point of view.

Vincent Van Gogh wrote to his brother saying that he would give anything for a particular type of crayon. He confessed that with this crayon he could draw great pictures. The photographer who thinks that he can take better pictures if he owns one type of camera or gadget has some support for his feeling according to Van Gogh. But, the man who thinks that equip-

9. This portrait of Vivian Fine, composer, was made with the 135mm lens.

10. This gauge was shot with the same lens as figure 9, but with the bellows extended to maximum. Thus, the use of a bellows attachment with a 35mm camera expands the range of coverage. The gauge is one inch high and the bellows permitted a 1:1 recording.

ment is the *end* of the creative process, will never be capable of doing anything except buying more equipment. The millions of cameras, lenses, films, and other accessories that fill the photographic gadget bags, have only one purpose: to aid in the production of better pictures and to extend vision. Anyone who loses sight of the meaning and use of his camera and equipment is losing sight of the goal of meaningful photography.

Very often it is the fresh point of view or new way of seeing that is possible with a new item of equipment, which will change a commonplace subject into an image never before seen. I have produced several photographic essays of rather ordinary, even cliched, subjects that revealed a fresh image through the application of a new lens, or housing, or bellows, or camera. The pictures of the Broadway actress, Elizabeth Ashley, and the Football Fathers, were given new impetus and meaning because both were undertaken with a newly purchased reflex housing for the *Leica*. And it was the obtaining of a bellows attachment, that further led to an extension of my camera craftsmanship. When I am making photographs, there are several cameras draped over my neck and shoulders. Someone once observed that I looked like a camera Christmas tree. But, regardless of appearance, I feel that I must have the right equipment or camera tool available for the right situation. I cannot afford to miss a picture because of wrong or inadequate equipment. And, nearby are all of the items that have specific uses for specific occasions plus new equipment that might lend fresh vision to old images.

One example of new equipment stimulating creative vision, and increasing the scope of my shooting range with the rangefinder 35mm, occurred due to the acquisition of a bellow attachment for the reflex housing. With this bellows I now use the 135mm *Hektar* to cover shooting distances from 1:1 to infinity. With the 135mm lens mounted to the bellows and reflex housing, I can copy a small document, picture an extreme close-up of a screw gauge, or show hands busy at work. Or, I can compress the distance of a large area. And finally the lens can function normally as it would with the rangefinder, except that it is now a single-lens reflex. Of course, the single-lens reflex 35mm's have the same feature with perhaps one disadvantage. With the single-lens reflex camera there is no need to purchase the reflex housing. The design of the camera eliminates the added expense.

Another feature that becomes important with the use of the bellows is the adaptation of off-brand lenses or surplus lenses. Once in a while a fine quality high-aperture lens may be bought, and with the aid of the bellows for focusing, may be adapted to your camera. I bought from military surplus an f:2.7 152mm lens for only a few dollars. Camera repair specialist Marty Forcher fitted the lens to my *Leica* bellows. It works beautifully and has given me another working tool in my chest of creative instruments.

Thus far I have been very general with regard to the many techniques of the 35mm camera that complement the creative talent of the photographer. Perhaps it would be unnecessary to get overly specific for some readers, but almost all photographers can profit by new information or a refurbishing of old information. Therefore, to accommodate everyone, let's now get into the techniques that apply to the thirty-five millimeter and enable the creation of photographic images from the latent to the enlargement.

MANY EXPOSURES POSSIBLE

Monet, of the school of Impressionist painters, would have been a great photographer. His ability to recognize and utilize the effects of color and of light were instrumental in his producing great and exciting paintings. His series on haystacks is probably as close to the thirty-five millimeter technique of recording many images of the same scene, taking advantage of the most minute alteration of light or elements, as we can get outside of a photograph. As the light would shift or change, Monet, who worked on many paintings concurrently, would put aside one painting and pick up another more attuned to the harmony of the light and scene.

The 35mm cameraman by rapidly, or in some cases slowly or cautiously, surveying a scene, recording even the slightest change, can accomplish what Monet was doing with his art medium. Of course, we can not return to a previously exposed film to improve upon it, but we can take full advantage of the devices of the camera or darkroom to improve each exposure, altering the visual concepts.

The one precaution that the user of thirty-five millimeter cameras must take is to avoid the temptation to over-shoot without regard for the pictures he is taking. The indifferent snap-happy shutter-snapper will burn up a lot of film and in all probability have nothing but a lot of film to develop. But the concerned and creative cameraman will explore the many facets of the subject and shoot no more film than the snap-happy individual. It is one thing to shoot a roll of 36 pictures without varying distance, lens, exposure, or angle. It is another thing altogether to expose a roll of film searching through different angles, lens lengths, or alterations of light and exposure for the *one* composition that captures unalterably the essence of the subject. I call this technique "visual notemaking." Just as a writer will make hundreds of notes compiling thousands of words from which he will glean the right combination of nouns, verbs, and adjectives to make his final statement, so the

11. Do not be afraid to shoot a lot of negatives. This picture of children and their chalk drawings, taken in Newburgh, New York, was one of many of the same scene. This picture combines all elements to best advantage.

12. Space and contrast may be combined to give the greatest possible impact to a subject. Used in an essay on youth, this picture contrasts the bigness of the world with the smallness of a child.

photographer must have the patience to explore every visual possibility of a subject to make the statement he wants seen. On occasions, the sum of the total is possible in one negative. But seldom is this true of photographers who use thirty five milli-meter equipment. Edward Weston could wait patiently for hours for the light to be in proper position before making one negative of a scene. The thirty-five milli-meter cameraman should have the same discipline to wait out the elements of nature, but he should never be satisfied to record only one negative of the scene. Film is much too cheap to risk failure in getting the right picture. The swiftness with which one may alter positions and angles gives the 35mm photographer ad-

vantages impossible with the bulky, bigger cameras. Not to take advantage of this mobility is not to use the medium to its optimum.

Photography, unlike most other art media, is a process of subtraction rather than a process of addition. In the me-chanics of the photographic process the tools of recording the images formed in the mind of the photographer demand that the image be smaller than in the original scene. In 35mm photography the recorded image is infinitesimal when compared to the original. We accept that our negative or color transparency will be an inter-mediate step toward the final print. Years ago when a picture of a large subject was to be made, a camera which would ac-

13. The space relationship is employed again to contrast youngsters with the building. A wide-angle lens assisted in accentuating this relationship.

commodate the size film needed to record the subject in a one-to-one ratio was constructed. The classic example is the camera that was built to picture a locomotive. The camera was the same size as the subject. The reason for the large camera was that a large picture was needed and enlarging was not yet a part of the photographic printing process. Today, enlarging is necessary. We, in the 35mm photography field, consider enlarging an integral part of the overall process.

We begin our pictures by reducing the scene to a one by one-and-a-half inch negative. The image is then projected to another size which is considerably smaller than the original scene. The process is very flexible. In the graphic techniques which are often compared to photography,

the final print is the same size as the main or master image. In larger camera operations the negative may be of a size to allow a contact print which is large enough for proper viewing. Not so in 35mm photography. Because of the fluctuation from large to small and back again, the composition of a miniature negative must be very tight and strong. If the composition is not strong, the reducing and enlarging will usually magnify the faults. For this reason the photographer must exercise greater discipline in the selection of the elements that will make up the design of his picture. To do this he must subtract the unwanted elements from the composition selected for recording. The picture is neither added to nor constructed as is done with every other art media, but rather the

14. A sunshade protected the lens from light-flare in the backlighted scene. A 50mm lens stopped down produced maximum sharpness.

15. Football Fathers. Achieving a compression of the players and the two men guided the composition of this picture. With the use of reflex housing, the image could be seen before the shutter was pressed.

picture is formed by leaving out all but that which is desired to create the visual statement.

In painting, the artist begins with a blank canvas. He constructs his picture by adding the color, design, subject, and other elements that express his intentions in the painting. The same is true of other graphic arts such as block prints, lithographs, silk screens, or woodcuts.

Perhaps the sculptor is the most akin to the photographer in respect to the creation of his image. The sculptor begins with a block of wood, stone, or other materials.

He then subtracts from the mass until the image of his mind is formed in the material with which he is working. But he has the advantage of being able to add to his work by reworking or altering.

The photographer is restricted in his recording of a concept to the instant of the film's exposure to light. The latent image holds that vision until chemicals activate and make it permanent. Some alterations, still of a substractive nature, may be made when the film is printed. But on the whole, the picture recorded is the picture complete. Darkroom manipulations can be employed to change the composition, but the content of the composition cannot be changed. There can be no building or reconstructing in areas when unwanted activity occurs. In short, the photographer must substract his final composition at the time of the exposure. He must also remember that some alterations can be made if necessary, but nothing can be added that is not originally there.

Seeing in photography has been a term which has lost its meaning because so many photographers who are incapable of defining the term, have attempted to define it. I am not going to be guilty of perpetuating the philosophy of the untalented. The art of any man is individual to that man alone. If others understand his image, the artist belongs to the world. But if the artist must tell his audience what he has created, there is little value in the picture. In photography, the camera-artist must be able to apply his tools as indicated by his visual sensitivity. Why he chooses one technique over another or one film over another is only significant to the mechanics of the medium. His ability to see, have insight into, or understand the subject before his camera, is solely his.

16. Newburgh, New York. The 50mm lens has a great enough angle of vision to cover most normal compositions. The depth of field is more than adequate at distances over ten feet.

17. The f:1.5 opening on the 50mm lens permitted this informal portrait of a Kenya student in the UN Security Council chamber. From the shooting distance of twenty-five feet, there was ample depth of field to obtain a sharp image of the huge room behind the subject.

And a person with a creative eye does not need a camera in his hand to keep his mind active in viewing the world about him. Cognizance of the many events that are performed about him keeps him alert to all activities and keeps his reflexes at peak performance in preparation for the next time the camera is in his hand.

In the contact sheets on page 35 are many pictures of Eleanor Roosevelt. Using a 200mm lens and with backlighting, I was able to "see" Mrs. Roosevelt in a fresh angle. Can you select the one picture which *The New York Times* used? The enlargement is on page 37. This series indicated that it is the individual using his own preference in mechanics and other elements of the photographic medium, plus his sensitivity, or seeing, that creates the pictures. And it will develop that the individual will discover his own style, or approach, to his work because of his preference for the tools with which he works.

ment and "leaded-pants" to try the amateur equipment. Perhaps his inability as a photographer would be discovered if he were removed from the studio where all pictures are made under the "thumb-tack" technique. The "thumb-tack" technique is a lighting arrangement formed by placing the lights over thumb-tacks stuck in the floor. Any deviation from these "thumb-tack" positions would confuse the cameraman completely. Do not misunderstand me. I have no complaint against the truly dedicated studio photographer. Many of them are currently using the 35mm camera for their work. What I do have a grievance against are the sheltered, out of date, big camera studio photographers who damn any equipment except the kind that they use. I was teethed on an 8"x10"; reducing to a 5"x7"; then to the 4"x5"; 2¼ square; before going completely to 35mm twelve years ago. I know the limitations imposed on the photographer by the immobile camera and equipment. I have experienced the loss of pictures because of my inability to move with the tide of activity. And I have lamented the lack of portability in the boxes of accessories needed to carry out my work properly.

With the 35mm camera, not only do mobility and portability cease to be a problem, but they are an integral part of the creative process. Several rolls of film, a different lens length or two, filters, and other items, may be carried comfortably in one's shoulder bag while at work. The tool to improve your vision or visual interpretation is as close as your elbow. The world traveling photojournalist, who is perhaps the most creative of all the thirty-five millimeter users, can embark upon a lengthy assignment with little more than a suitcase and a camera, with a gadget bag

on his shoulder. It would be hard to imagine having to fly half-way around the world with the massive equipment required of the studio-stranded photographer.

On an assignment to photograph two of the top executives of Central Hudson in Poughkeepsie, New York, I took along two *Leicas* and three lenses. One camera was equipped with the reflex housing and 135mm lens. The other M-2 body was altered with a 35mm wide-angle and a 50mm lens. I was granted a one hour session with the men and I had to get a variety of pictures intended for several uses by the public relations department. The visual variations possible with the different lenses offered some changes. The natural lighting of overhead fluorescent and daylight suggested changes through lighting. The most important factor was that I was almost immediately in rapport with my subjects. They were interested in the way in which I was working and in a matter of minutes they became involved with their own conversation and forgot about me. Their responses to each other produced natural and revealing pictures. I shot seven rolls of thirty-six exposures each in the time alloted. The average exposure was 1/30 at f:4. I used Plus X film. By taking the camera to the subjects and working in their familiar surroundings, I was able to gain contact and response from the men that would have taken a long time to acquire, if it were achieved at all, in the studio.

With all other factors being equal, the thirty-five millimeter photographer would have the edge over all other photographers because of the mechanics of the medium. The design of the camera, the fast shutter speeds, the fast lens, the interchangeable

18. The problem here was to place the lone female in equal position to her male co-workers. The 200mm lens focused on her and used with a wide-open aperture emphasized her face alone.

SHOOT 360 DEGREES

The creative photographer who is in command of his equipment and cameras has but one objective: to make the very best pictures he is capable of. This includes the extension of the photographer's ability beyond his working techniques. Creative urges often project the artist-photographer into new experiences. Sensitive photographs demand that the photographer have compassion for the people and subjects he photographs. Curiosity must prevail to the extent that the subject is seen in as many ways as possible.

Unquenched curiosity determines the selection and recording on film of people and places. The method which I endorse, to assure that all possibilities of the subject are explored, is the "360 degree" look. The technique is simple but the results can be tremendous. The subject is circled, as

you look and picture the angles, designs, and lighting that contribute to the idea you are trying to photograph. Complete circumnavigation of the subject will eliminate the possibility of missing a good picture because you did not look for it. The act of circling the subject could be called photography's cubism technique, for the total viewing of a situation requires seeing it from the top and bottom as well as from all sides.

MOBILITY AND PORTABILITY

The 35mm camera has often been given a second-rate position in the professional world by untalented photographers who call themselves professionals. But the truth of the matter is that the so called professional is not a proper judge and is too weighted down by his stationary equip-

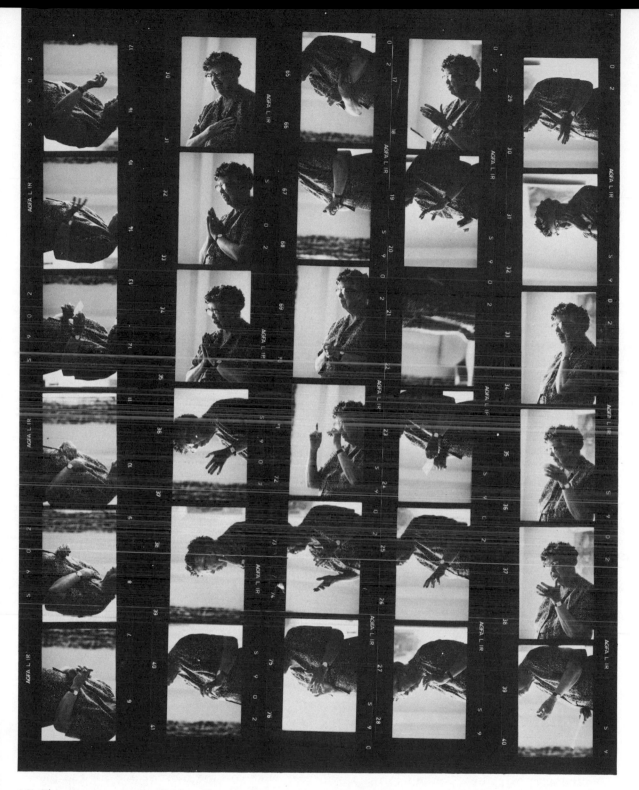

19. This contact sheet of Mrs. Eleanor Roosevelt was shot by available light and with a hand-held 200mm lens. Can you select the one frame *The New York Times* used? (See figure 21.)

20. An assignment for *America Illustrated* on the fun of family skiing produced this head and glasses shot. By using the 135 mm lens and stopping the lens down to f:32, maximum sharpness held the image of the reflection as well as of the man's head. Close composition accents the eyes.

lens gamut from super wide-angle to extra long telephoto, are the unequaled variety of choices which give the thirty-five millimeter cameraman a keyboard of creative instruments unexcelled by any other format. Whether he learns to render a concerto or only masters the basic scale is up to the man, the artist. If he is capable of mixing his mind, eye, and camera into a combination, functioning toward creating photographs, the 35mm format will broaden his creative scale.

I cannot accept the excuses of some of my colleagues that *everything* has been photographed. Perhaps everything has been photographed, but as long as I am physically able to explore and experiment with my 35mm camera, I cannot help believing that there are still untouched areas I have not pictured. I will continue to look for the fresh, the different, the image that only I can see. If you can convince yourself that you too must search for the picture that only you will see, you will be a better photographer.

21. Mrs. Eleanor Roosevelt, a portrait. This picture was used with an article in *The New York Times Magazine* on the occasion of the seventy-fifth birthday of the world's first lady.

22. Mike in the Woods, 1959. A year-long essay on a two-year-old.

SEEING IS THINKING

Since the camera is a device for recording the thought waves of the photographer, I am fully convinced that the act of *seeing* is the act of thinking. Often the camera has been called the recorder of the mind's eye. The eye of one's mind is the thought. Therefore, I feel strongly that a photographer should *think* pictures and he will *see* pictures.

Unless the photographer is willing to do some mental exercises to activate brain cells to become observant of the world, he might just as well not put film in the camera. There is no mental energy required to copy or imitate a picture which has already proved successful. All that is required of the photographer is that he preconceive the composition and go about finding that composition. If he has seen the original in a book or on an exhibition wall, the task is made easier.

But, if the man desires to find something new to be said about an old subject, he must put to work the capacity he has for thinking. With a little sincere thought and concern, almost any competent camera technician can convert cliched subjects into exciting images. In this chapter we are going to explore the year-long essay I photographed involving my own son and his second year of life. I have chosen this essay for discussion because the subject is typical of material available to nearly every photographer in the world. There is probably a child in the family of every photographer. Seeing or thinking out a series of pictures of such a readily available subject will generate activity in your mind. The camera claims these thoughts on film.

By being constantly aware of my son Mike, by watching his every activity, and through the wide choice of camera mechanics, I documented the life of a two-year old as seen by his father. For variety in points of view, different lenses were used. For texture variation, different films were used. For accentuation of activity, the print was controlled. No device for strengthening the design of the composition or power of the subject was left unused. A creative act or series of acts must never be controlled by the mechanics of the medium. Dictation of the creative control must come from the mental elasticity of the brain behind the camera.

23. Mike, 1960. In picturing my son for a period of one year, I was able to employ full use of equipment, lighting, and other devices to strengthen the visual statements. A subject so close at hand is a genuine challenge to one's creative seeing.

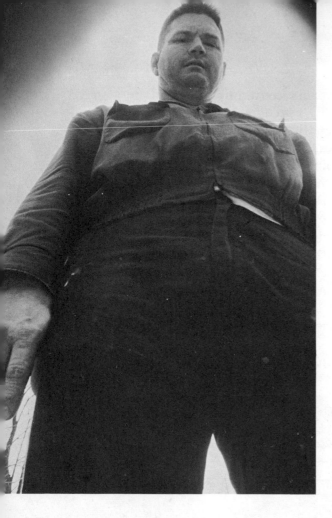

24. This is the elongate impression that Mike has of me as he gazes up from his boyish height. The giant of "Jack and the Beanstalk" could not be more startling.

25.-27. Mike. This is a sampling of the hundreds of pictures taken of my son. Lenses from the 135mm to 35mm wide-angle were used.

28-29. Seeing is thinking. The commonness of a subject demands that the photographer's mind be active to find the ingredients that make exciting pictures. With a subject as close at hand as one's own child, there is a challenge to discover the many picture possibilities that exist.

30.-32. These three pictures were made with a camera resting on the dresser top facing the mirror. Mike and I mimicked as I made the pictures. A wide-angle lens helped assure reasonable sharpness.

33. The elongated shadow in contrast with the tiny figure of the boy symbolizes the relationship of adult and youth.

A CAMERA AT ALL TIMES

I believe that a photographer should have his camera with him all of the time. Not that he will be taking pictures at every turn of a corner, but should the urge to record a scene occur, the instrument for the creative act—the camera—should be handy. How can you expose a film of a composition that stimulates your creative sensitivity unless you have the camera with you? I have an old *Leica* IIIA with an f:3.5 *Elmar* 50mm lens, which I carry at all times when I am not on a particular assignment where I would normally have all of my cameras. If I leave the house for a walk to the supermarket, the camera is hung over my shoulder just as unconsciously as my overcoat is donned.

Anyone who thinks that just because he carries a camera constantly, he will score a major photographic coup is only deluding himself. Just as expensive equipment does not make the photographer, so the fact that a camera is in your hands does not guarantee good graphic documentation of a subject. Adequate or even simple equipment used by a sensitive individual will produce far greater images than the most expensive equipment in less creative hands.

A man who was in charge of the department where I once worked told me that he could not see how I could picture the subjects I did with the sensitivity and involvement I entertained in the compositions, because I looked too much like a football player. I did play football as well as all other sports, but my physical ability does not have anything to do with the sensitivity of my mind to the reflex of my finger in the act of releasing a shutter. There is no such thing as a physical image of a person with a creative mind. The bearded bohemian or sneaker-wearing person with an emaciated, thin physique could both house the minds of creative geniuses. So could a five-by-five frame with a moon shaped face. A man's talent cannot be judged by his physical appearance.

Having the camera with you at all times will encourage an acute awareness of everyday events. Surprisingly enough, you will suddenly discover the excitement and interest in people and scenes that have long been so close to you that you failed to see them.

The technique which I use in carrying

34. The super wide-angle 21mm Angulon focused on the child, six feet from the camera, was stopped down to f:11, and everything from two feet to infinity was in focus. This is depth of field at its optimum.

the camera constantly is the hyperfocal distance setting of the focus and lens. Later in the book I discuss fully the theory of hyperfocal distance, but let me apply it here with a partial explanation. I use Plus X film if the day is one of sunshine or typical daylighting. The exposure is determined by a meter reading. In selecting the lens opening, I choose the smallest opening to match a reasonably fast shutter, as with 125th at f:16. I set the infinity mark on the focus scale opposite the f:16 on the far side of the focus calibration. To determine the closest point of focus, check the position of the depth of field f:16 on

the focus scale. For the 50mm *Elmar*, the depth of field range would be six feet to infinity with the point of focus falling at about twenty-five. You need not focus the camera so long as you are working within this range, as everything will be recorded sharply. In effect, the camera is functioning as a fixed focus or pre-set camera.

If you are shooting fast, or shooting subjects of unusually rapid change, a fixed focus camera will enable you to shoot with concern only for the subject. The camera is not a burden or hindrance, and it certainly ceases to demand any attention on your part except to advance the film.

35 -37. Three examples of why one should have a camera at all times: the quiet peace of a Christmas sleigh ride, the thumb-sucking of a nursery school tot, and a street scene are spontaneous, never-repeated events.

All of the pictures shown in this chapter were taken with the techniques described. And while some of them at the time of exposure did not fit into any story or essay, they have later become parts of published magazine stories.

PART II

Theories and Practices

ON HONESTY

Across the desk sat Yoichi "Oke" Okamoto of the U.S. Information Agency. He was looking through my portfolio. I nervously twisted a pencil. I am always nervous when people look at my pictures.

Oke looked up, "You are a very honest person, aren't you?" he asked. I nodded yes. "I can tell, because it is obvious in your pictures," he continued. "And that is an admirable characteristic."

Okamoto did not realize it but he had paid me the greatest compliment anyone can pay. Honesty is the one element in my photography that I treasure most. The word encompasses a multitude of philosophy in seven letters.

But what is honesty in photography? Does it mean unposed candid shooting? Is it unretouched negatives? Does it include directed situations? Can an honest picture lie? Is cropping cheating?

To answer these questions I make some comparisons. In the field of ethics one can read the works of great philosophers who devoted their lives to defining the word "good." Men like John Stuart Mill, G.E. Moore, and Saint Augustine wrote many words relating their thoughts on "the good." While there is merit in each man's theory, there is still some argument about the definition of the word good. This is in some degree the situation surrounding the word honesty in photography.

Everyone who ventures an opinion regarding his definition of honesty in photography has merit in his statement. Cartier-Bresson[1] believes in the decisive moment as his revelation of honesty. W. Eugene Smith,[2] who often recreates situations, says that he does not create rules

[1] Henri Cartier-Bresson *The Decisive Moment.* Simon & Schuster

[2] W. Eugene Smith, Former Life Photographer

47

so he does not live by them; the picture is the ultimate end. And these men are both honest photographers.

The combination of both of these approaches to photography is another pattern of thought. There is, and always will be, room for the highly directed (i.e., the movie script), decisive moment. And this too is honest, because it is telling a planned story that can be either fact or fiction.

An honest photographer can still render a dishonest statement with his pictures. At the 1957 University of Miami Photojournanlism Conference, a man told of his experience in portraying the worst side of a heavy-weight politician. The editor of the newspaper was opposing a politician and wanted to show him as a big fat slob. A highly ethical photographer was assigned to picture the man in off-guard moments that pointed toward the editor's theme. Everytime the politician opened his mouth to eat, talk, drink, or yawn, our honest photographer was there to record it. The photographer was making honest pictures. But, when the editor added his caption, the photograph did not make a truthful statement. The photographer had been quite truthful, yet even he had waited for those moments when the politician was not his usual self. While in this case the pictures were unposed, they were dishonest. Would it be correct to deduce that photographic honesty must include making unposed pictures?

I believe that honesty in photography depends upon the mental attitude of the photographer. If the man is honest in his approach, then his pictures will be honest. Should the man prefer to observe the record, then posing his pictures would be incongruous with his character. But if the man feels that rearranging or recreating a scene will tell the story better, for that man, posing is permissible. However, if a man has no firm convictions on which to base his thoughts, he is likely to be dishonest in his pictures no matter how he exposes his film.

Exposure of the film does not conclude the question of honesty in pictures. There is a furthering of the honest picture idea in cropping, either in the printing or the layout of a publication. By altering the original context of the photograph, a new concept can be created about a subject.

A famous investigation in Washington, D.C., was a prime example of this type of untrue statement brought about by cropping. A photograph taken of several people disembarking from an airplane was cropped to include a smaller number of people. This photograph was then used to prove that two of the men in the picture were acquainted with each other. Who lied? The photographer was honest in his recording, but were the others who handled the photograph?

Oke handed me my picture portofolio. Then he gave me some suggestions for stories I could do for him. As I rode the bus to New York that night, I reflected upon our conversation. How was I honest with my photography? Was it really that obvious? I know that I like to be the observer and recorder always looking at my subjects with uneditorialized eyes. Yet on some rare occasions I will undertake to direct my subjects into recreated parts to be acted for the camera. Both of these procedures produce photographic purity.

Sometimes a client will assign a project which he wants handled according to a prearranged, preconceived idea. His idea. How can a photographer honestly handle such an assignment unless he is allowed to rearrange some of the prearranged? When a photographer takes a job such as this, he is not an artist seeking to speak visually, but rather a puppet with a camera and a load of film.

Just as G.E. Moore, the philosopher, is concerned with the indefinable "good," so I am concerned with the indefinable "honest photography." Does it exist? Is it in degrees for the mass, and only complete for a few? Or does it really matter except to the artist? For the sensitive mind, it most certainly does matter. John Stuart Mill, although speaking on "good," sums it up ably for the concerned photographer: "It is better to be a human being dissatisfied than a pig satisfied."[1]

IDEAS FOR PICTURES, SELF ASSIGNMENT

No amount of reading or thinking about pictures will substitute for the actual making of pictures. If you do not put into practice the knowledge of photography you have, how can you ever expect to produce pictures that are good? Or how can you expect to improve upon your past work? Making pictures tends to create a curiosity that results in the exploration of new and better techniques, or the fuller use of known techniques. One method of insisting to yourself that you make pictures is to assign projects to yourself.

In camera clubs the monthly competition is designed to do the same thing, but I have witnessed many club competitions and very few of them satisfy the creative urges of creative photographers. Usually, there is a mutual admiration society at the club and no one, unless he is an outsider, will truthfully criticize the pictures. The results are perpetually bad pictures. There is bad choice of lighting, no stimulating handling of subject, and worst of all, bad print quality. In the end, the monthly assignment projects fail to stimulate the club's members to create quality pictures. For this reason and for the purpose of forming an atmosphere of creativity about yourself, I propose that every photographer should have his own assigned projects, with himself as his most severe critic. The projects need not be of a great time consuming variety; rather they should consume your thoughts to such a degree that your eyes are always open and your camera always handy.

But what kind of self-assigned projects will help to apply my knowledge; learn new techniques; and apply old techniques to greater creativity? This is a question that perhaps every reader will now ask himself.

The following photographs constitute a list of twenty projects which you can assign yourself. Each of these has applied one or more of the techniques or theories discussed throughout this book. The picture accompanying the assignment is one which is intended merely to show what can be done, and not how to do it. Only your imagination should be the means of selecting the picture to fulfill the assignment.

1. Abstract a familiar landmark.
2. Backlighting for depth.
3. Use a screen wire for star effect.

[1] Great Traditions in Ethics, American Book Company

38. This is another attempt to show the many sides of Miss Ashley. For an actress to have reached the heights which she has achieved, the energies of four people would be required. By the use of mirrors, several images of Miss Ashley were placed on one negative. A wide-angle lens helped maintain sharpness in the depth of coverage.

5. Let motion be used to strengthen movement.
6. Use close-up for detail.
7. Humor.
8. Nighttime.
9. A child's world.
10. Use a foreground framing.
11. Outdoor portrait.
12. A picture story of one stationary subject.
13. Unrelated objects in a related theme.
14. The designs of snow, rain, or nature.
15. Composition in use of large areas of space.
16. The feeling of loneliness.
17. Use of one light for total lighting.
18. Indoor portrait with studio lights.
19. A landscape with backlighting.
20. A portrait with existing light.

There is not a professional photographer worthy of the title who does not undertake creative projects for the sheer sake of producing pictures of which he is proud. Photojournalists very often undertake independent productions (not to be confused with shooting on speculation) of subjects which are of considerable concern to them.

Perhaps a story idea is so intangible that word outlines fail to convey the idea and pictures are needed to sell the subject. This was the case in the essay I did on Elizabeth Ashley. The girl was a young, unknown theatrical hopeful who had been signed to do her first Broadway play. I

39. Elizabeth Ashley, 1961. One light on the stage was the only source of illumination for this portrait. At the time, Miss Ashley was unknown on Broadway. By the absence of detail I portrayed her as an anonymous symbol. A Leica Summarit with a f:1.5 lens setting was used for an exposure of one-fifteenth of a second on Plus X film.

40. Abstract a familiar landmark.

41. Backlighting for depth.

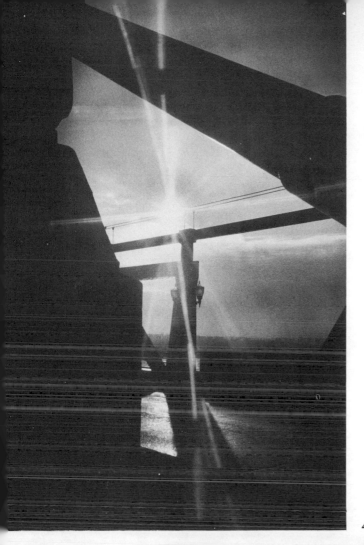

42. Use a screen wire for star effect.

43. Give feeling of texture.

44. Let motion be used to strengthen movement.

45. Use close-up for detail.

46. Humor.

47. Nighttime.

48. A child's world.

49. Use a foreground framing.

50. Outdoor portrait of Ronald Howard.

51. A picture story of one stationary subject.

52. Unrelated objects in a related theme.

53. The designs of snow, rain, or nature.

54. Composition in use of large areas of space.

55. The feeling of loneliness.

56. Use of one light for total lighting.

57. Indoor portrait with studio lights.

Not every self-assigned project imposed on oneself will be as successful, yet the sum of many projects will be the production of better pictures. As you are challenged by an assigned idea, you begin thinking of how many ways you can approach the theme and how many different pictures you can make. To a degree, it is like playing *Scrabble*. The letters are juggled until the tiles form the maximum number of words with the maximum count. In the process you will find a number of combinations which are good, but not the best. In approaching a picture idea you will find many ways of photographing a subject or theme, but not all will be as good as you are capable of finding. The best work will come through a process of elimination, through shooting everything to which you react. By shooting many negatives using many ideas, you will find the right combination of ingredients that will create the picture you will be proud of. The total shooting should contain several very fine pictures. These pictures could be identified in much the same way as sketches and drawings are rendered before a painting is begun. Then the product of the many images produces one image.

Camera clubs could undertake the self-assignment idea on a very large scope by initiating a project such as picturing the historical value of the town in which the club operates. Or the club could do a civic job of documenting the activities of *The League of Women Voters,* the *Lions Club,* or the police force. By making the project large enough in scope, every member of the club could find people and things to photograph. As each member is motivated, he will make pictures that will contribute to the project, as well as contributing to his own growth in applying

had no idea of how this actress would be different from other young actresses. Yet, after talking to the girl, I was convinced that she was a very animated subject and worthy of the investment of time and expense required for a photographic essay. I did the story and *Pageant* used the material, as did *The Saturday Evening Post,* and several foreign magazines.

The self-assigned project allowed me to create some exciting pictures which found their way to the pages of top magazines.

58. A landscape with backlighting.

59. Mary Margaret McBride, 1962, a portrait with existing light.

his knowledge of photography.

The more you can challenge yourself to take pictures, the better the quality of your pictures will be. Ideas and the carrying out of these ideas are the foundations of creative photography.

ON PRECONCEIVED IDEAS

When one approaches an idea with a preconceived image of what that idea should produce visually, he must try to *explode* that image and replace it as the parts are picked up and placed into compositions. The assemblage of the many parts should be accomplished through the selection of functional bits that produce the whole. The bigger the explosion of the preconceived idea, the better the reassemblage will be. The more ingredients or parts there are that one has to select from, the better the chances will be of succeeding. Unless the mind is willing to destroy the subjectively formed images predetermined by the background or environment of the individual, that mind can never function creatively. One must be willing to destroy in order to create. In photography we destroy the subjective to create the objective image. Granted that nothing is truly objective, but the approach to the creative act must be done with the presence of a mind willing to overcome all personal pride, passion, and prejudice, if these things conflict with the honesty of the image.

ON CROPPING

The thirty-five millimeter photographer was once referred to as the man with the postage-stamp negative. With today's trend to issue the oversized commemorative stamp, the comparison is even closer in actual dimensions. The one inch by one-and-one-half inch negative is not much larger than the Project Mercury, four cent stamp. Because of the smallness of the negative format of the 35mm, the photographer must make every effort to fill the frame with his composition. Utilizing the most minute area of the frame could save headaches in the darkroom in an attempt to get something worthwhile from the composition. The large format photographers might consistently circumvent trouble by being able to discover a useable portion within the twenty to thirty-five or more square inches of the negative. But the 35mm photographer who shoots with the thought of second guessing is pressing his luck and probably accelerating his trip to disaster. The one-and-one-half square inches leave little to second guess. Even if there *might* be something within the frame's design, chances are it will be so small that the quality of the image will be destroyed or impair the image impact on the viewer when the enlargement is made.

It has long been my practice to print the 35mm negative in exactly the way it was exposed. I cultivated this habit when I first used an 8"x10" view camera. Even when I reduced the negative size to 5"x7", 4"x5", or the 2¼" square, I still printed full negative. The discipline learned in these negative sizes was carried over into the 35mm format, when twelve years ago I abandoned all cameras in favor of the thirty-five millimeter. Today discipline of my using the full frame is a second nature reaction.

I would never say that pictures must never be cropped. Very often a radical for-

60. Roping a Filly, 1956. This is a full-frame print. By the positioning and use of space, this picture appears to be longer than it is. Panning increased the feeling of motion.

mat created by cropping will make a dramatically strong picture from an ordinary design. However, there are always exceptions. The creative person will never allow restrictions to impose themselves if that imposition lessens his creative range. I believe very strongly that the photographer should become a master of his space to a point of seldom requiring reconstruction of his picture's composition by cropping. If the discipline of filling the 35mm format is imposed on the individual by himself so strongly that he thinks in the format shape, the pictures he takes will contain the exact ingredients necessary to full and

complete compositions. The demand to fill the frame will become an unconscious motivation and will dictate the selection of the elements of composition that will fit the format.

When the compulsion to compose in the shape of the 1x1½ inch format reaches the point where every picture is conceived in that shape, the photographer is ready to take advantage of the technique of cropping for impact. In all probability the picture's design will be interesting in its entirety, but for a dramatic departure from the conventional, a radical shape formed by cropping could improve the subject. To afford the luxury of cropping, the photographer must first master the technique of full frame composition. By constant practice of always printing his pictures in their full frame as originally exposed, the photographer will see and be able to study the good as well as the bad compositions. He can study each roll with a dedication to improving his technique of picture composition. Very little knowledge of composition is needed to tell when a picture is really bad. Pictures that are strong in construction are easy to see. The contact sheet of a 35mm roll of film enables the study of a full shooting and the best pictures can invariably be spotted. The poor ones are also obvious.

The criticism most often offered about the 35mm format is that it creates a sameness in a group of pictures as might be seen in an exhibition or a book. I recall a very heated debate I once had with a few photographers. One of the members of the group stated that she felt that I *did* crop my pictures because they all seemed to have a shape compatible with the action within the composition. After assuring her that I *did not,* except in extremely rare cases, alter my composition at all, I asked her to point out a picture that supported her statement. She selected the picture of the boy chasing the girl, opposite, and said that she was certain the picture was longer on the horizontal than the usual 35mm format. We measured it and proved that the picture was in exact proportion to the negative. The critic's counter-statement was that the picture seemed to be a different shape, and this I contended was in part due to the manner in which the subject was placed in the format. The action suggests that the picture is wider than it is, and the motion enhanced by the technique of "panning" accentuates this feeling. The value of my critic's observation lies in the reenforcing of my theory that a strong discipline of design, within the full format, will permit the photographer the freedom of selection that strengthens the subject. By understanding the space he has to work with, he will use it to greater advantage.

While it is advisable not to resort to cropping when working with a 35mm negative, there are times when the pressure or restrictions of shooting leave no choice. Perhaps the lack of a long lens restricts moving in close to the subject. Or a quick shot disallows getting in position for the proper placement of the subject. Cropping for strength in printing would be necessary, but, if the photographer has been consistently capable of utilizing his frame, he will know in advance how the finished picture should be cropped. His training will pay off in a stronger cropped composition. In such a situation the subject is not being haphazardly handled, but selected from the photographer's experience in using space properly -- space, in this instance being the area in which the subject is located with other areas having no effect on the design, because they will be eliminated, as they are being eliminated mentally during the shooting.

There would be an explosion which would shake the art world if painters were consistently guilty of stretching large canvases on which they would paint their most expressive images, and then cut the painting down to include only a fraction of the original picture. There is hardly a painter who is worth the price of his paint who would consider doing this to his work. This practice would be frowned upon by critics and artists alike. Yet, the practice of cropping of a negative by photographers is not only approved of, it is encouraged. The discipline of the painter in using the fullness of his canvas should serve as a directive for the photographer.

One last observation regarding cropping which does not necessarily apply to the technique of taking the picture. When a selection of pictures is being laid out as for a magazine, book, or exhibition, it is often desirable to select from a photograph only small parts of the total field composition. The whole of the layout is made up of parts of pictures. This application of cropping the photograph is without malice, for the composition being created in the layout is the process of selecting the right ingredients to make a statement of meaning. Forming a layout composition is the technique of selecting, just as forming a picture composition is a process of selectivity. But this is not second guessing to salvage a composition. This *is* the composition.

VISUAL TEXTURE

Through high quality optics and camera mechanics, it is possible to record graphically maximum detail in a split-second. The quickness with which the lens retains all it sees makes use of a device of design which I call visual texture. From infancy we are concerned with texture. We feel things as we explore the world about us. The roughness or softness of a surface causes a pleasant or unpleasant emotional response. By transferring the ideas of texture to visual terms, the same responses may be produced. The term visual texture is not new. Many photographers refer to the design of a picture as the pattern. However, if the pattern is a part of the picture's composition, it may be more than just a repeating design.

There are two forms of visual texture. One is the mosiac type of design and the second is the tactile type of design. Applying either of these two devices of design creatively requires understanding of their meaning.

A mosaic type of visual texture is created by an overall breaking up of the photographic format into small areas. While it is not always necessary or required for effect, the shape and size of the mosaic texture technique is the same or near the same. The picture on page 71 of the man climbing a rope has a mosaic type visual texture. The shape and size of the spacings of the net form a pattern and establish a foreground, giving meaning to the man and the background. A visual sense of depth is created by the design of the net.

All mosaic styles of visual texture do not come under the foreground application as seen here. There are patterns formed by the repeating bricks of a wall, shadows that speckle a sidewalk, dark objects on light backgrounds, and, conversely, light objects on dark backgrounds. These designs may be used as background, to direct eye travel into the subject, or for contrast or complement of the picture's composition. There is no end to the ways and means by which the mosaic technique of visual texture may be applied. The simplest of structures may be turned into strong contributors to compositions when converted to textural functions. The variety of adaptations is as broad as the photographer's ability to recognize them.

The second type of design is called tactile texture, because it is usually formed by a subject that contains a suggestion of surface that one would know by touching. A pile of concrete pipe or blocks, if photographed for the texture of the material, would be geometric in construction of composition, but at the same time would have a strong visual sense of the roughness of the material.

When the actual texture of a surface is considered important in the picture, it is necessary to use lighting to accentuate the material giving feeling to the texture. Backlighting, sidelighting, and crosslighting are the best choices of light when maximum detail and textural feeling are desired. It is not often that the mosaic design is dependent on the quality or kind of light for its function. But with tactile texture there must be a sense of touching the material, and lighting is very important in establishing the mood or attitude of the mind. Light conditions the eye to see and feel the texture of the composition. However, it is not necessary for the texture of the material to be included for the geometric application of visual texture to apply. The shadows of a picket fence cast on the ground and diminishing in size to infinity form a geometric texture without the tactile feel of the subject. To interpret the idea of geometric texture, you must first understand that anything that forms a composition in a repeating pattern design is geometric texture at work. If there is the added feeling of the surface of the subject photographed, you have placed a second element in the picture—tactile texture.

There is only one method by which a physical application of tactile texture can be applied to photography. This method utilizes the surface of the sensitized paper. In painting, the paint has a texture which can be exaggerated by piling the paint on the canvas. This combines a physical texture with the pattern design of the composition. The photographic paper which has a pseudo-textured surface may be used for creating a sense of surface with a visual texture design. For example, there are surfaces of paper that imitate the sensation of touching silk, tweed, canvas, suede, and tapestry. A silk surface could give a sense of touching the material of a wedding gown, or a tweed surface might accentuate the tactile sensation of a portrait of a man. However, these surfaces are not at all recommended to "doctor" pictures. Use them with care; and use them cautiously, being sure they contribute to the theme of the picture.

TRAVEL WITH YOUR CAMERA

The general impression of the American tourist is a slightly over-weight, beret-topped, camera-covered man of about forty years of age. The cameras he carries are of the thirty-five millimeter variety, slung bandolier fashion over each shoulder. He wears a blanket-weave sports jacket and smokes cigars. He seldom takes pictures. One has only to travel in Europe on any summer day to witness this description in a living, breathing being.

The dedicated photographer intent on making creative pictures during his travels will seldom be identified by his appearance. Since the 35mm photographer's greatest asset is being inconspicuous, he will do everything to remain anonymous. The camera is often hidden under his quiet colored jacket or raincoat, being brought into view only when pictures are to be taken. The additional cameras and lenses are on hand for his use, but are not on public display. The creative individual wants to remain unnoticed, while he participates and photographs activities. The best and most authentic travel pictures are made with unobtrusiveness as the key characteristic of the photographer.

For the sake of identifying a working procedure, let us undertake to explain a typical situation. If you appear on the streets of many towns in the world bearing two or more cameras over your shoulder, the kids will swarm all over you asking for gifts. Many adults want to be paid for having their pictures taken, and even if you pay them, the spontaneity of the scene is often shattered. On the other hand, if you keep your camera handy but concealed (or at least protected from the curious), you will be free to walk the streets causing little or no interruption in the daily activities of the people. You can employ the hyperfocal distance-shooting technique to pre-set your camera, eliminating the fuss of preparing the camera. With the hyperfocal distance and lens and shutter in agreement, your only concern is the selection of the compositional components that create interesting statements. After a few exposures, your presence may become known, but by then you will have succeeded in recording the honesty of the situation as you have witnessed it.

One of the best ways of becoming a part of the scene, whether in a foreign country or a new town in your home state, is to disguise the fact that you are a photographer. Amateur photographers tend to make a display of themselves. Perhaps this is their goal and taking pictures is less important. However, if taking quality photographs which are meaningful and important is your objective, the camera must be handled without fanfare. This means that the extra accessories which usually are carried in a shoulder bag should be out of sight. In such a situation, I prefer to wear a big coat and load the pockets with the necessary film and extra lenses. If the pockets are big enough, the bulges will not show. Additional space can be gained by removing the film from the boxes.

BRACKETING THE EXPOSURE

In traveling, many picture situations are encountered that are very interesting. To preserve these striking scenes and situations, the pictures must be made immediately. To assure successful negatives and transparencies of this situation, you must take several pictures using different settings. This type of insurance shooting is known as "bracketing the exposure." After determining the exposure with the exposure meter and the exposure made for that combination of lens and shutter, you change the lens, shutter, or both to increase or decrease the exposure. A range of three stops above and three stops below the meter reading will cover all variance in light, tone, contrast, and mechanical deficiency.

For example, if the meter reading suggests an exposure of 125th at f:16, you would also shoot 1/60th at f:16, 1/30 at 16, and 1/15 at f:16. And you would shoot three exposures 1/125 at f:11, 1/125 at f:8, and 1/125 at f:5.6. You could also combine these if desirable. If 1/15 of a second is too slow, you could shoot 1/30 at f:11 for the same results. In effect, what you are doing by altering the exposure settings is assuring yourself that at least one of the negatives or transparencies will produce the correct quality image that you want.

61. Picnic, Hopewell Junction, 1961. When traveling, look for interesting pictures to be made. The camera set for hyperfocal distance enables a quick recording of fast-changing activity to be made.

Perhaps more than one will be correct, and more often than not many of them will be good. But when you are traveling there is little chance to return for a re-shooting. Or if you do return, the conditions may not be as interesting. Professional photographers can not afford the luxury of mis-

sing, so they bracket their exposures in excess of their need for pictures. The expense of returning, if returning is possible, far outweighs the additional film investment.

Bracketing is not to be confined to those who travel. The technique is one which you should employ any time that you must secure the very best quality negative or color transparency possible. Obviously, with this technique there is always the possibility that you will have a few missed exposures due to under- or over-exposure, but that is expected, for the aim is to get the right combination of lens and shutter which will be found within the wide range possible in the bracketing of the exposure from the median.

If you are traveling overseas as a non-professional, there are certain regulations that you should be aware of. For example, the quantity of film is often restricted to about ten rolls per camera. And two or three cameras is considered enough. If you carry more, there is always the possibility that they will be confiscated until your departure. If you want to try your luck at taking more than the allowed film, distribute the rolls throughout your luggage. However, film is reasonably available in all countries. Black and white films offer little problem, for you can usually locate a film that contains the approximate characteristics that match the film you are accustomed to working with. In color, the problem is a little more acute. Since most photographers dislike switching color films because of the shorter latitude found in the color emulsions, it is advisable that the same type of color emulsions be used. Locating the same emulsion color film is not always possible overseas. This is true whether you are an American going to

Europe, a European coming to America, or a Japanese going to Africa.

Kodachrome and *Eastman* films have about as near world-wide distribution as one can find and even these are not always available. The best safeguard against running out of film is to carry all you are allowed. You can send the film for processing as soon as it is exposed, which means that you could have additional film sent to you if you are located at one address for any length of time. A call to your local postmaster will help answer questions about sending film anywhere out of the country.

Professional photographers also have their problems. When they enter a country they are allowed to bring all of the equipment and supplies necessary, but getting the equipment out may not be as simple. The only method of proving that all of the equipment is yours and was brought into the country, and not purchased there, is to register it as you enter that country. For that matter everyone should register his equipment as protection.

What are some of the procedures which one should follow and techniques that should be followed as photographs are taken while traveling? First, if a lengthy trip is planned, whether overseas or a motor tour of the U.S.A., the fact that it will be a major undertaking suggests a picture story treatment of the entire episode. By putting the "start-to-finish" of the trip on film, many exciting pictures will result. If you do the story in color, you have a well prepared travelogue to show your friends, or perhaps you may sell it as a travel story, if professional photography is your aim. All of the events of the trip are photographed as any picture story would

be. From the large total of pictures shot will be selected the few pictures that are the most important of the trip. By approaching the trip from a story-telling point of view, a little more freedom of interpretation is possible.

You should be able to use one or all of the techniques of motion, selective focus, hyperfocal distance, screen wire or other devices over the lens, all forms of lighting, and grain to make the many situations visually vibrant. Since few trips are not major undertakings, is it asking too much to reward yourself by photographing the project in its entirety for later enjoyment? In this way you will reap the additional rewards of more meaningful pictures.

One suggestion for shooting while traveling which is not a procedure you would use often, but which could enable photographing a subject which otherwise would be missed is shooting from moving vehicles. For instance if you are traveling on the British Railway System and the landscapes are attractive but you cannot stop, try shooting from the window of the moving train.

Shooting from the window of a moving train is not difficult, but there are a few precautions which should be taken. Remember, the camera sees in much the same way as does your eye. If you look at an object as you approach it, the object is sharp while the foreground and background are unsharp because of the movement. Therefore, a scene that is to be pictured is more sharply photographed if you shoot with the scene in front of you. The same thinking applies to a scene that is behind you. If the train has a rear observation platform, you can shoot very sharp pictures of the scene behind the train while the train is traveling forward.

Secondly, scenes in the distance are more easily recorded from moving vehicles than closer scenes. To eye test for the way in which the camera will see the clearness of the scene, all you need do is look at the same area with concentration on the part that the camera will see. If the area is racing by, the camera will see it the same way. The technique of "panning" is employed in a case like this if a central subject is desired sharp while the other areas "move."

The camera should be your constant companion when traveling. Travel and photography combine two of the greatest American pastimes. They could combine for great pictures.

62. The net creates a pattern of mosaic-type visual texture as it breaks up the total field of composition.

63. The stone wall forms a mosaic framework to isolate the tiny figures in the background. A wide-angle lens assisted in retaining the sharpness.

64. Bennington, Vermont, 1960. The perspective of the fence established another type of mosaic texture.

65. The backlighting of the sun helps to give a feeling of texture to the snow. This is one form of tactile texture.

PART III

Taking the Pictures

HOLDING THE CAMERA

Lack of sharpness in 35mm is usually the fault of the photographer. Pictures of quality and sharpness are possible with even the very low priced cameras. And, of course, highest resolution and optimum definition are possible with expensive cameras and lenses. Yet, unsharp images occur with both. The capabilities of the equipment are not at fault. Very often, if the one who is quick to accuse and shout damning remarks about the tiny negatives would stop to consider the human element involved in the shooting of the picture, he would probably not say a word. Slight fuzziness or double image is most often the result of not holding the camera still at the moment of exposure. (The lack of sharpness as applied here is not to be confused with the special and specific technique of creative imagery through unsharp and motion compositions.) There is nothing more unneces-

sary than a ghost image when only one image was intended. The shaky hand can be blamed for this.

There are three practical and workable methods of holding the 35mm camera, including using lenses up to 400mm. The pictures illustrate the methods. Try them all and select the one which fits you most naturally.

Gripping the camera properly, the second important contribution to a steadier hand while shooting is the technique of breathing and releasing the shutter. In the army, we were taught to fire a rifle with the method: aim, deep breath, release half of the breath, relax, take up the slack on the trigger, squeeze the trigger. If this technique is modified and applied to the shooting of a picture, you will have a process of focus, deep breath, breathe out, compose, take up shutter slack, squeeze shutter. Naturally, this act is ridiculous and unworkable if you have to think about

74

66. To support the weight of the telephoto lens, place the elbow and arm close to the body, pressing against it. The triangle formed by the hand on the camera and the arm against the body will safely support the hand holding the long lenses. Wrap the neck strap around the wrist for additional rigidity.

67. To support the normal weight of short-length lenses, the strap can be wound around the wrist, but is not necessary. The arm should be pressed against the body and the camera firmly held in the palm of the left hand. With this technique, exposures can be held up to one full second.

68. If optimum support for the camera is needed, take a squatting position. Wrapping the neck strap around the wrist, hold the camera as shown in figure 66 and brace the elbows against the knees. This is perhaps the maximum support possible without the use of a tripod.

69. This 400mm telephoto shot of a street scene was hand-held for a fiftieth of a second by using the technique illustrated in figure 66.

70. There is greater assurance of detailed sharpness if the camera is firmly held during the exposure.

each of these maneuvers as you take a picture. The only way for the procedure to serve its proper usefulness is for you to practice the method until it is done automatically. The method should never impair the major asset of 35mm photography which is quick and easy mobility of the equipment. After a short practice session, you should be able to use the shooting technique with the speed with which you have always handled your camera. But there will be a greater chance for sharper pictures due to a steadier held camera.

The three techniques of holding the camera—using the neck strap wrapped around your hand, the elbow against the body when shooting with long lenses, and the camera in the palm of the hand, combined with the techniques of releasing the shutter will not guarantee that all pictures will be absolutely sharp, but the chances are that greater sharpness will result. Remember, if critical sharpness is necessary, by all means plan on using a tripod whenever feasible.

of unnecessary damage to your film, do not rewind the film any further into the cartridge than the "leader" which is exposed when you load the film. Many cameras have an indicator to show when the film is dislodged from the take-up spool, which is the time to stop winding. For cameras that do not have indicators, you can listen for the slightly louder sound as the film pulls free from the take-up spool.

Not only does leaving the "leader" of the film outside the cartridge protect against undue scratches, but it also gives you a place to make notes about that roll of film as to exposure data, subject, development recommendation, etc. This feature can be of major importance when you shoot a lot of film before processing. You can well imagine your dilemma if you exposed ten rolls of film in a day or two under a number of lighting conditions and with a number of different ASA ratings, if you had not marked each roll. By putting the notes on the film's "leader," the notes are never misplaced or forgotten.

ON SCRATCHES

Scratches on 35mm film can be prevented by not completely rewinding the film into the cassette. If the film is rewound into the cartridge, the film continues to roll tightly until taken from the camera at which time the spool spins freely, allowing the film to unwind within the cartridge. If dust or other foreign matter lodges on the film as it enters the film cartridge when the film is being rewound, the tighter the film is wound, the more damage the foreign particle will do to the film's surface.

To safeguard against having this kind

SOME THOUGHTS ON LIGHTING

The usual breakdown for defining lighting in photography is high key versus low key. And the usual definition for these two categories is that high key is basically white and gray, while low key is basically black and dark gray. Both are correct. But to be able to understand the working meaning of these two extremes in handling of light intensity for the photographic process, one needs to know what happens to light.

Perhaps it would improve the explanation if we first discuss the "use" of light. In the word "use," I am not applying it to

71. Harry James, 1957. An f:1.5 lens allowed full advantage to be taken of the one spotlight in the night club for this on-stage portrait.

the act of exposing film. I *am* applying it to the creation of images through the eye to the brain and later, through the lens to the film. To use light, you must first be aware of light. And to become aware of light requires only that you observe the universe around you. The brilliance and warmth of light can create warm, happy thoughts and pictures. The absence or coldness of light can convey images of loneliness and/or abandonment. The sun can be used to produce both effects. Artificial lighting sources can also produce these effects. And both kinds of lighting can form lighting levels in varying degrees of the two extremes.

The more light you have to work with, the more detail will be produced in your pictures. Greater light enables wider control of the lens setting and shutter speeds. Depth of field and sharpness are under more flexible control with the abundance of light. Since higher intensity of light allows the use of a slower ASA film, you will gain increased linear sharpness and higher resolution power. And yet the picture need not be a high key picture when using a lot of light.

High intensity of light only allows for a wider selection of elements to construct a picture. The depth of detail, the tempting textures, or the vastness of coverage, plus the unlimited control of the ratio of light which is used to place emphasis on the subject, are contributing factors and control the final picture. The photographer has the choice of how much or how little will accentuate the texture of a plane. The position of the light in relationship to the camera will control the viewer's response to the subject. And the light versus dark areas will establish the mood that the scene will create for the viewer.

The ratio of light to dark tones is, of course, established by the quantity of light. The exposure of the film can be used to influence the ratio. For example, if the room exposure is used, the relationship of light to dark will be in the middle gray of the scale. If the exposure is above normal, the relationship of light to dark (black to white) is greatly separated and results in a composition of predominately lighter color and would be called high key. Conversely, if the negative is below normal, the underexposure will reduce the middle gray and compress the black to white ratio, resulting in a low key scale of color.

The source of light whether indoors or outdoors makes no difference when working with the ratio of light. The important element is the brilliance or strength of the light. For the "key" of the lighting is determined by the brightness of the highlights when compared to the weakness of the shadow areas. For example, if the light source is very bright and records at 100 foot candles on the exposure meter, the shadowed area must register fifty foot candles to create a 2-1 light ratio. If the highlights register 100 and the shadows twenty-five, then the ratio of light to dark tones is 4-1. You measure the ratio by reading the highlight areas and then dividing the reading of the shadow areas into the highlight reading. The same procedure applies if you are using the sun outdoors, photofloods, or other artificial light indoors. The difference in technique lies in the greater control you would have with artificial light.

When using artificial light, you can usually regulate the ratio of light to dark by controlling the strength of the light sources. The highlight or main light which illuminates the whole scene establishes the upper light level. The shadows are illuminated with another light source which is usually called the fill-in light. The light level of this light source can be controlled by the intensity of the light, the distance from the area being photographed, or by diffusion. The intensity of the light may be regulated by the wattage of the lamp. If the main light has a wattage of 500, the fill-in light could be 300, and at the same distance from the subject the ratio of light to dark would be 2-1. If the lamps of both lights are the same wattage, you can control the light ratio by setting the fill-in light at a greater distance from the subject. The intensity of the light may also be controlled by placing a gauze or fiber diffuser over the light. If the light source is diffused with one thickness of diffusion material, it is the same as cutting the wattage in half. Of course, if you are using an exposure meter, you can measure the ratio of intensity of each light by first turning on the main light and reading its foot-candle brilliance. The fill-in light is turned on after the main light is turned off, and the meter is used to measure the strength of the fill-in light. At this point you adjust the shadow light for the desired percentage by either of the previously mentioned techniques.

When using the sun as the light source, the only practical methods of balancing the light ratio are the use of a reflection or fill-in flash. Both have disadvantages, but are invaluable when needed. The reflector system of illuminating the shadow areas is perhaps the easiest to work with and certainly the easiest to see in action. Any reflecting surface such as a white card, aluminum foil, white painted plywood, or even a newspaper, are effective reflectors. The sunlight is bounced into the shadow

areas which require added light. The degree of brilliance of the reflector is determined by the reflector surface and the angle it has to the sun. The movie industry employs reflectors to assist in the lighting of scenes, even very large scenes.

The use of flash, whether electronic or bulb, is a more portable shadow fill-in source, but at the same time a little more difficult to use. To determine light ratio with flash, you must first establish the actual exposure for the light available. Let use assume an exposure of 1/100 at f:16 is called for. The distance from the camera to the subject being pictured is eight feet. You are using a flash source which has a flash factor of 145. If you divide the eight feet distance to the subject into the flash factor, you have an f:stop of eighteen. The light of the sun and the light of the flash are almost equal, or a 1-1 ratio. If you want a 2-1 ratio, you must diffuse the light of the flash by fifty percent. Other ratios are also established by adjusting the intensity of the flash, by altering the distance of the flash to the subject, or by diffusing.

These are workable techniques that every genuinely dedicated and creative photographer must know. Even if the techniques are never used in these rather tightly controlled applications, the 35mm photographer must learn all he can about lighting. Only by knowing lighting in all of its forms and variations can the creative eye search out the lighting that complements the vision of the mind.

To this point we have concerned ourselves with lighting that the photographer has at least limited control over. But the 35mm photographer is more inclined to seize upon the available lighting prevailing at the scene and record his impression as stimulated by the effects of the light playing on the subject. The technique of lighting for the available-light photographer is not so much the control of the light, but the selection or recognition of the light. The effects of light as it etches images into the mind can be faithfully seen by the camera lens if the photographer understands fully what is taking place with regard to light-to-dark tonal relationship.

The eye has a much wider range of sensitivity to light than does the film emulsion. Very often the eye will see detail which is impossible for the film to record. It is the ratio level of light-to-dark tonality that makes it possible for the film's sensitivity to record the picture as seen in the mind.

SHOOTING INTO THE LIGHT

If I had to choose one light source as my favorite, the choice would be back lighting. With this style of lighting, the camera is aimed into the light source and the subject being photographed is between the camera and the light. Outdoors, the subject is placed between the sun and the camera, creating strong shadows and a burst of light that commands attention from the viewer of the picture. Light rays can cause streaks across the composition resulting in dramatic imagery. Of course, most often the main subject is rendered in silhouette or at best contains limited detail. Yet because of the startling effect, the missing detail is permissible.

Indoors, or under artificial lighting, an effect similar to sunlight can be accomplished by shooting into the light source. Stage lighting, natural lighting, or a bare bulb can be employed effectively to achieve the same unique light and shadow designs possible with the sun.

But, it is very hard for anyone accustomed to having the light fall over his shoulder to break an old habit and try something entirely new in his experience. For that reason, perhaps it would be well that we discuss the technique or mechanical process required for successful shooting into the light source.

There is no need to use any other film than the one with which you are familiar. The exposure will be determined by the speed of the film and according to the intensity present. I am a strong believer in an exposure meter, and an evangelist for the use of the meter in lighting conditions of unorthodox situations. In reading the light value for shooting into the light source, there are two ways the light may be evaluated. One is to aim the light sensitive cell at the light and shoot for the maximum highlight. The dark tones and shadows will lose all detail and possibly the fringe gray will lose detail. But the strong highlight areas will record faithfully and tonally true.

The second technique of using the meter is to read the light reflecting from the medium gray area and thereby hit a norm of light value. You may do this for an overall scene or a close-up by holding your hand so the light hits it in the same fashion as the subject is being lighted. Read the light that hits the back of your hand. The light reflected and recorded on the meter will be equal to the middle, or near middle, gray scale of tone. You will record the tonal range in the middle gray from the darkest to the lightest areas. And you will retain detail in all three areas of tone. If detail is important, this technique

72. Elizabeth Ashley, 1961. Very often the absence of light will yield interesting pictures. The emptiness of the theatre and the solitude of the girl are accentuated by the one light and the mass of black. (Taken for *Pageant Magazine*.)

73. Henry L. Scott, an informal portrait. Shooting into the light source is a technique which every creative photographer must master. Strong and dramatic effects may be accomplished by showing the brilliance of the light. This picture of Mr. Scott is given added impact by the strong light just above his head.

74. The glow of the light outlines the figure in this night shot. There is no doubt as to what is to be seen because the lighting controls the journey of the eye.

75. Rim lighting is possible when the light source is employed behind the subject. This sledding composition is made stronger by a line of light outlining the figure.

76. Mardi Gras, 1950. The flare of the lights enhances the feeling of the night parade.

will produce the results you want. Of course, you will probably have slightly overexposed the highlights which will require additional "burning-in" when the print is made. Possibly the shadow area might not be as strong as you might wish and require some additional control to retain detail in the print, but since the total creative process certainly includes the print procedure, you must allow for some work to be done in the darkroom.

Shooting into the sun or another light source does not guarantee that you will gain immediate success in your pictures, but attempting this, or any other untried technique, *will* mean that you are willing to experiment and in turn learn more about the creative character of a fascinating medium. It means that when you master the exposure technique, and understand the objectives of dramatic lighting, you will create stronger pictures.

PEOPLE TO PEOPLE

The 35mm camera and its wide selection of lenses and other accessories makes the best equipment for photographing people. No other equipment can offer the photographer the facilities with so few inhibiting factors. The camera is mobile enough to enable hand-holding when speedy and responsive candid portraits are the requirement. The need for rapid operation is very often demanded in formal as well as informal approaches to portraits.

77. Ernest R. Acker, Central Hudson Gas, Poughkeepsie, New York. This formal portrait was made in the office of Mr. Acker. There was no posing or lighting arrangements. After observing the natural position and play of light, the picture was made with a 135mm lens.

78. Clark Gable, 1957. This informal portrait was taken with an 85mm lens during a brief lull in the making of a movie. A dozen pictures were made in less than five minutes from several angles.

79. Terry Moore, 1957. Hotel room lighting was used for this warm portrait. A 50mm lens wide-open took full advantage of the light level.

When time or subject allows for the use of more control and more typical techniques of studio portraits, the 35mm camera on a tripod can produce as fine a quality portrait as any camera on the market. Plus the fact that a thirty-six exposure roll of film permits enough shooting without reloading to insure maximum chances for success.

If very close-up, penetrating portraits are wanted, a wide-angle or normal 50mm lens might be used. If the subject is somewhat inhibited or you want to remove yourself from the subject, a choice of telephoto lenses allows variety of images from full head to full length, and you can still remain some distance from the subject.

Of course, the choices of various lenses are also available in the conventional view-type portrait camera, but this type of camera is not portable. In fact, it is so heavy that it must be mounted on a dolly-type stand. There can be very little spontaneity between photographer and subject when the camera is no more maneuverable than a small truck. The type of film used in the conventional studio camera is big and bulky, causing many lost minutes of shooting time while the individual film holders are being clanked in the camera. A full roll of thirty-six pictures can be shot while four pictures are being made with the studio type camera. Is it not easily understood that better pictures can be made when you are shooting fast and that you will have a higher percentage of useable pictures? The greater selection of exposures will most assuredly guarantee a better choice of expressions. When the lighting has been carefully arranged and all other important details of posing, clothing, etc., have been attended to, it seems

80. Tommy Sands, 1958. Again, hotel-room lighting was the only source of illumination for this picture. Taken during a news conference, there was no time to arrange posing or lighting. A 90mm lens at f:4 helped bring the figure closer from a shooting position across the room.

pure folly not to shoot enough film to get the very best picture possible. In the 35mm technique the cost investment for a roll of thirty-six exposures is less than six to eight exposures in the large conventional studio size camera.

Perhaps the photographing of children is best accomplished when using the 35mm camera and lenses. I know several very fine photographers who employ the 2¼ format in their work and with excellent

81. Earl K. Long, 1954. After waiting thirteen hours in the halls
of a hotel, I was able to get an hour with Mr. Long to make pictures for *Time Magazine.* Because of the quickness with which
lenses and shooting angles may be changed, nearly 200 pictures
were taken.

results. I cannot help wondering how
much better the selection of pictures
would be if there were thirty-six pictures
shot instead of twelve. I should think the
results would be more than three times
better.

There are two techniques most recommended for photographing children. Both
are good and neither is recommended over
the other. So, let us discuss both of them.
The rangefinder type 35mm with the eyelevel viewing is best used without a tripod
or any inhibiting of movement of the photographer. Lights should be positioned in

a square design so that wherever the photographer moves, he will have an interesting lighting effect.

The square light arrangement is one
which I feel is best for getting the most
when photographing children. The technique is simple but effective. It requires
four lights of equal wattage. The subject
is placed at least six feet from the background. A light is placed behind the subject on the right and left about five feet
away. Two more lights are placed in front
of the subject, one on the right, one on
the left, and both at five feet. The lights

82. Joan Brandon, an informal portrait. The make-shift stage was lighted with sixty-watt bulbs which were replaced with #2 photoflood lights of 500 watts. This picture was shot during a demonstration on hypnotism. The light of the match under the hand is complemented by the bare bulb overhead. (Taken for *Look Magazine*.)

83. Barbara Lekberg, sculptress, 1959. In portraiture, some attempt should always be made to include related objects as a part of the compositional design. In this picture the sparks of the welding are not unlike the lines of the wire of Miss Leckberg's construction.

should hit the subject with equal intensity.

The exposure will be equal no matter where the photographer moves. Yet there are many styles and designs of lighting possible with this technique. If the photographer stands by the light to his left, he is shooting into the light on the right rear. This can produce a combination front, side, and backlighting effect. Shooting from directly in front of the subject will produce a well balanced frontal light with highlights being cast on both sides from the two backlights.

More dramatic effects of this basic arrangement can be accomplished by moving one light in front and one light in back and closer to the subject. By altering the distances of the lights to the subject, the ratio of light intensity has been changed and the relationship of highlights to shadow will be widened. For example, if the right front light and the left rear light are moved one foot, the lights will be stronger and will produce stronger highlights. The lights which are not moved become fill-in lights, keeping the increased shadow transparent. Also, there can be a combination of relocating the lights. Both back lights can be moved closer, as can both front lights. Of course, exposure will change as either of the lights is moved, so be sure to check the new light value.

REFLEX IN PORTRAITURE

The principle of the reflex design in 35mm is excellent for picturing babies or adults. By seeing the subject through the same lens that you will be using for recording, the composition will be stronger and the action of the subjects easier to follow. And you have the option of putting the camera on a tripod or hand-holding.

If you prefer the camera to be in one spot while you move about the subject, getting him to look away from the camera, you will want to mount the reflex 35mm on a tripod. The height of angle, focus, depth of field, and the lighting may all be studied in detail for the effect it will have in the reduced format of the one by one-and-a-half inch negative. By the use of a long cable release or vacuum release, you may venture away from the camera's rigid position to attempt getting a more relaxed image of the sitter. Care must always be taken, when undertaking the shooting of subjects where camera and subject are stationary and the photographer mobile, that the subject does not move out of the picture range. This is an all too common fault when the camera is placed on a tripod.

Unless you stay at the camera, peering into the reflex housing, it is very possible the subject will move from the desired composition. The single-lens reflex attachment on the thirty-five millimeter gives much of the advantage of the view camera in the approach to portraits, but adds the value of more pictures-per-minute. The prism reflex with the eye-level viewing is

84. Arthur Kopit, 1961. This young author and playwright is very relaxed and rather carefree. This aspect of his personality is accentuated in the portrait.

B

85A. Rim lighting with a newspaper reflector to fill in shadows. The light is two feet above the model's head.

85B. Side or hatchet lighting, half highlight, half shadow. The light is at the same height as the model.

85C. Butterfly or Hollywood lighting; the shadow beneath the nose identifies it. The light is three feet above the model.

85D. Rembrandt lighting; a triangle of light on the shadow side identifies the nose. The light is at the same height as the model.

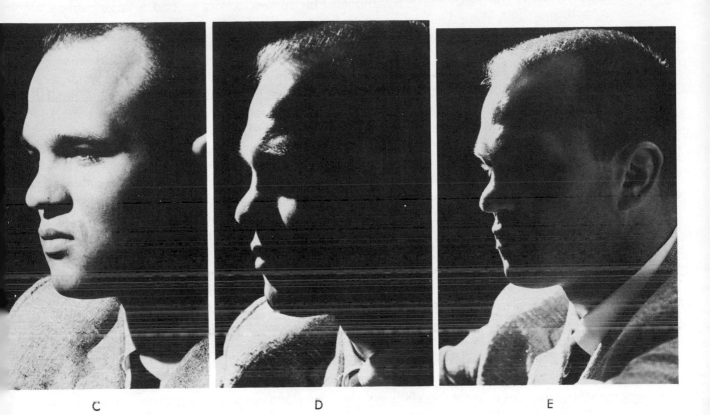

C   D   E

85E. Rim lighting without any filling of shadow. All five of these pictures were made with the light source in one position. By relocating the camera or by turning the subject, who also remained stationary, various lighting effects were achieved. Each of these effects may be gained with existing light. It is not the lighting equipment, but recognizing the lighting effects that is important in portraiture. These same effects are possible with a street lamp, reading light, spotlight, or flood light. (Model: Joseph Orze, Murfreesboro, Tennessee.)

All lights are of the same wattage and at an equal distance from the model. All lights may be used at once or in any combination. Variations in effects will be accomplished by pivoting the model, combining the lights, or revolving the camera around the sitter.

very close to the rangefinder techniques of shooting with the added advantage of seeing the image exactly as it will appear when projected to the film's sensitive surface. A trifle more freedom is afforded the user of the prism finder 35mm than is possible with the rangefinder camera. Usually the prism finder will focus closer and, for many people, more accurately.

Again I wish to advocate strongly that you never judge the creative application of a piece of equipment by the opinions of someone else. The camera that works best for you might very well be the item that your best friend has condemned. Tools of creativity are only functional in the hands of the person who has the proper respect for the equipment and its operation. If you have any doubt about the right choice of camera, give it an honest test before discarding it as unworkable or unwanted. If you have never tried 35mm techniques in portrait photography, do not condemn the product until you have given it a fair chance to show its worth. I have used the rangefinder, single-lens reflex, and prism type 35mm cameras with satisfying and stimulating results.

NUDES AND GLAMOUR

The use of the 35mm camera has only recently been applied to the photograhing of the beauties of the world. There was a time when a photographer of beautiful females would not dare approach his subject unless he had a large camera. The twin-lens reflex 2¼ square was considered a small camera. But the qualities of increased shooting per hour and greater mobility prompted the glamour photographers to test the merits of the small camera format. The 35mm proved itself. Today the use of the 35mm camera to portray the most beautiful faces and figures of the world is highly acceptable.

Actually, there has been an interesting freshness injected into "pretty girl" photography due to the use of 35mm techniques. Again the greater selection of lenses allowing closer and more intimate views has enhanced a series of glamour pictures. Also, more exposures without the hampering of reloading assures a better selection of pictures. And color shooting has become economically feasible. In both the photographing of the figure and glamour, the techniques that belong exclusively to the 35mm are creatively applied. A series of nudes I produced employed excessive grain by the use of fast film and over-developing to accentuate the grain structure, making the figure composition resemble the texture of granite. The beauty of the picture was in the structural form and texture which complimented the gracefulness of the figure.

The 35mm equipment allows excellent glamour and nude photography to be made in improvised conditions. The usual studio lighting and props are not necessary. The light and props of the average room are sufficient. The shorter length lenses permit working in very close quarters. And the medium-long length lenses enable out-of-focus of unwanted backgrounds. It is not impossible to consider

86. Probably the one field that 35mm has not begun to dominate is that of the glamour and nude. Techniques and qualities are equal to those of other formats, but photographers have not yet begun to use the 35mm camera. This glamour shot was taken while the model was preparing for other pictures. It is the best of the entire shooting.

87. The nude above was done in the home of the model. A series of pictures was taken employing photojournalistic techniques of lighting and of freedom of posture and movement.

that very interesting and creative glamour pictures could be made in the usual size room. In fact, I have made pictures of celebrities who were traveling and would only permit pictures as they lounged in their hotel room.

Many of the pictures I did on the Elizabeth Ashley story were taken in a small hotel room where she lived temporarily until her play opened on Broadway. All of the color was shot by the light of one window on a very overcast day. By utilizing the color of curtains and mixing daylight with artificial light, good color tones were obtained. All of which is intended to suggest that you do not have to have an elaborate studio to put your 35mm camera to work effectively in the field of glamour photography.

STAGE PHOTOGRAPHY

There are a great many restrictions and demands placed on the photographer if he seeks permission to photograph a play or stage performance. Very often he is relegated to a distance not to his liking and informed that no additional lighting is permitted. If the photographer has a press-type camera, he is in trouble. But a telephoto lens on a 35mm camera which can be hand-held comfortably, will usually have an f:stop enabling the use of stage light to satisfactorily record the action. There are very few instances where the light level of a stage will be so low that good, even lighting will not exist. An exposure meter reading for overall illumination is the best technique for stage shooting.

Regardless of where the action takes place on the stage, the norm of light value will permit taking pictures. And when the shift of full lighting of the stage to one spotlight is made, the exposure is altered very little, but the details of the stage are lost and you have a person suspended in depthless black. The picture of Art Carney on page 59 shows this kind of lighting. Effective use of space for dramatic impact of the subject may be achieved by the placement of the figure in this black mass. In the picture of Claude Rains, the feeling of projecting to an audience is accomplished by putting Mr. Rains in the lower right corner and the large mass of black to the left.

The technicians who skillfully light the action of a stage production make a tremendous contribution to the photographer. By recognizing and using their talents, the photographer's job is made considerably easier. The thirty-five millimeter photographer has another advantage in that he can fully explore the effects of lighting by exposing scores of negatives using different compositional constructions. The more creative the person, the more ways the same light can be tried.

FORMAL AND INFORMAL

Generally speaking, there are two approaches to photographing people. One is the formal or studio type with controlled conditions. The other is the informal, uncontrollable, and perhaps unpredictable

88. Claude Rains, a portrait. With the aid of a 135mm lens, Mr. Rains was pictured while on the stage. It is not desirable to photograph anyone on stage, but if there is no other occasion, employ any technique of film, camera, lens, or composition to get the most pleasing picture possible.

approach. Both have their uses and merits.

The thirty-five millimeter photographer of adults will seldom be forced to choose between the large camera and any other equipment. If he uses 35mm, he will use it all the time. There are certain elements of a 35mm negative which must be taken into account when photographing adults. Retouching of unwanted lines and marks on the face is impossible without preparing an intermediate large negative. If this is not a factor and *all* lines will remain, there is no problem. The other usual objection is that all of the negatives will have to be enlarged to at least 2″x3″ for inspection by an untrained eye. Few people can appreciate the tiny images of a contact sheet of 35mm nega-

tives. But, with these two problems settled, there is absolutely no change of procedure in shooting formalized portraits with maximum control of lighting, subject, and camera operations with the usual studio cameras and techniques. You do have the advantage of using or not using a tripod as the subject allows.

There are several lighting techniques and these are explained in the section on lighting.

One technique which I like to employ when photographing adults in a formal arrangement is to seek a prop such as a chair or stool on which the subject feels comfortable. The lighting is arranged for the greatest compliment to the face and overall composition. This arrangement is then fully explored. Without altering a thing, I then begin to move about the person looking for unusual or different effects that were not seen from the original shooting angle.

Very often by shifting slightly in either direction, the lighting becomes more dramatic and the subject more interestingly portrayed. In fact, it is the shifting of position and moving in or away from the subject, altering the beginning arrangement, that will explore the subject to its optimum. The 35mm, with its greater mobility, permits this quickness of moving and recording and affords the photographer the advantage of searching for the significant picture. The uninhibiting factor of the 35mm assists the creative mind to function uninterruptedly, taking full advantage of each impulse.

With the exception of the controls that the photographer relinquishes when he turns to the informal approach to his subject, there is little visual difference in the results. The photographer must have a greater awareness of the effect of light and its importance. Since the photographer has no control over light, he must position himself and his camera to take advantage of the light-play on the subject. There is no attempt to direct the subject, and this demands a higher reflex response in the photographer. If his timing is off, the pictures will probably be good but not great.

09. Elizabeth Ashley, a portrait. Do not forget the impact of the ultra-closeup. The strain of emotion is fully visible in the picture of Miss Ashley as she learns the lines of a play. A 90mm and reflex housing allowed a view of the fully composed picture at the time of exposure.

A fast halfback who is out of shape loses the keen sense of timing so necessary if he is to elude his would-be tacklers. The quickness to start and the ability to fake at the right moment are lost because his coordination between mind and muscle are dulled. Since a photographer's talent is measured in fractions of seconds, it is easy to see that his greatest contribution to creative images is his responsiveness. His *timing* is more important than the film in the camera. The elusive characteristics of another person before your camera defy you to freeze them in light-sensitive silver. The victory will be lost if you are less than effective in response to the most minute change of position or expression. A moment unrecorded is a moment lost.

The informal approach to photographing people permits the photographer to remain separate from his subject. In the beginning the photographer has the choice of whether he wishes to become close to his subject and establish rapport, or whether he wishes to be an observer only, and remain as anonymous as possible. Both approaches are valid. It will depend on the subject being photographed as to which approach will be selected. Again, the wider selection of lenses and equipment will allow freedom of movement of the photographer without restricting his thinking. The primary objective in the informal approach to portraiture is to grab "out-of-time" a combination of characteristics that present the subject in the honest image. This is accomplished by taking full advantage of the photographer's knowledge of the subject, his effectiveness in handling his equipment, the recognition of lighting and its contribution to the subject's personality, and the mental calisthenics which enable the keenest response and reflex in answering the mind's demand to act.

It will surprise many fine photographers to discover that the lighting techniques that are formally arranged in a studio are also created by existing lighting in any room or area. For example, the light of a street lamp overhead can produce a glamour or butterfly lighting on a face. The same is true of any overhead light. Sidelighting, backlighting, and crosslighting, are all possible with lighting that exists in any room.

Beautiful effects may be achieved by using window light. These are formations of light and shadow patterns created by lighting, over which the photographer has not exercised any control, but which he could create with lights if he wanted to do so. His only effort in using them is the recognizing of the desired effect and the calculating of correct exposure to activate the film. The 35mm photographer is more of a user than a controller of elements. Creatively, his greatest asset is his ability to recognize complementing features and characteristics which he isolates in the architecture of his picture.

MULTI-IMAGES IN THE EXPOSURE

The collage is a respected form of fine art. We in photography can accomplish the collage effect on a single negative by multi-imagery through reflection and double exposures. The effect, plus the montage techniques, may also be produced in the enlarging and darkroom process and we will discuss this in the chapter on darkroom procedures.

90. Fifth Avenue, New York, 1962. The collage and montage techniques are easily achieved with the camera. Because the lens is able to render sharply all it sees, the real and unreal can be combined as the camera instantaneously records. The assemblage of real and unreal, related and unrelated, light and dark objects is easily accomplished because of the technical capabilities of the camera. This shot was made with a 21mm super-wide Angulon lens.

By using reflecting surfaces, the photographer can combine like or unlike objects to compose a dramatic relationship of subjects in a study of design and form. For example, if you face a store window which is reflecting the images of people on the sidewalk over the mannequins in the window to create animate versus inanimate human shapes, you can expose for the reflection and pick up detail in both the images. Always expose for the darker subject or image when shooting reflections. By selecting the exposure based on the darker tones, you can be assured of detail in the low key area and the highlight areas will seldom be overexposed beyond a controllable range. If the highlight areas are the most important, additional exposures should be made, bracketing the exposure to assure yourself of one negative that fits.

The juxtapositioning made possible by shooting reflected images makes it probable that one picture will tell the story that several pictures would otherwise be required to tell. That one composition will sum up a theme which would be impossible with several pictures. In his excellent *Statue of Liberty*[1] essay, Bruce

1. *Pageant* Magazine, December, 1959, "Spotlight on a Statue," pages 134-139.
   35mm Photography Annual, 1960, "Statue of Liberty," pp. 114-117.

Davidson utilized the reflected scenes of the statue to combine the structure with related subjects, or contrast the structure with unrelated subjects.

When shooting into a reflected surface, there is usually a slight increase needed in light that is exposed to the film. You should open up the lens a half-stop to allow for the additional light.

Reflections in water are handled the same way as reflections on glass or other shiny surfaces. Because the light is entering a surface and is being projected out, the light is reduced and will require some increase in exposure. For this kind of shooting, bracket the exposure setting. Inspect the results to see what additional percentage was needed and note the increase for future use.

Employing mirrors for double or combined images is a useful device. Several effects may be accomplished through the use of mirrors. You may get a repetition of the same image; you could have a reflected subject with relationship to the environment; or the real subject could be displayed with relationship to the reflected surroundings. As long as there is enough light, mirrors may be used to pick up whatever areas you feel necessary.

The problem of focus is perhaps the most acute one when shooting mirrors. What do you focus on? My rule is always to focus on the most important single element of the composition. If additional sharpness is required, the depth of field is consulted to determine how much I should stop-down the lens to assume focus in all areas. If, on consulting the depth of field scale, I find the lens being used will not produce the sharpness necessary, a shorter length lens is substituted. For example, if a 50mm lens will not give the sharpness wanted, a

91. A color transparency printed as a negative produced an interesting picture. Placed in the enlarger and exposed in the same way as a negative would be printed, the positive transparency produces a negative print.

35mm wide-angle is used. With the change of lens, a closer or different shooting angle might be required. Conversely, if sharpness is not wanted and a more out-of-focus effect desired, a longer length lens might be put to use. The selection of lens and the amount of sharpness depends on the idea within the picture and the photographer's carrying out of that idea. Exposure will be based on the f: stop needed for the depth and sharpness. Determining the exposure will be done the same way as previously mentioned in the paragraph on window reflections. Of course, an exposure meter should always be used to assist in selecting the right lens and shutter combination. Then if you are in doubt, shoot several frames bracketing the exposure.

The double imagery of the double exposure is a creative technique that allows the combination of images possible in no other way. The technique of double exposure is not complicated. Most 35mm cameras will permit double exposures. Some such as the *Leica* require the cocking of the shutter without advancing the film, while others require winding the shutter manually. Still others of the semi-automatic cameras which have manually operated shutters require nothing more than the usual operational procedure without advancing the film. If you do not know your camera well enough to use the double exposure, read the instruction book again or see a dealer for additional tips on the operation of your equipment. But find out how to shoot double exposures, for the technique can be a highly effective creative tool.

The exposure requirements for double exposures depend on the subject and the product of combined images wanted. As a rule of thumb, the less important image is exposed first and is slightly (about one stop) underexposed. The stronger, more important image is exposed last at normal exposure. However, if double exposures are made out of doors with an abundance of light, it might be well to under-expose the first image by two stops and the main image by one stop to avoid over-exposing the film beyond printable range. Over-exposure is the greatest problem when shooting purposeful double exposures. Here again, as a new technique, the recommended practice is to shoot several compo-

92. A window reflection of a cardboard girl and a parking lot creates a bit of fantasy. A 400mm lens compressed the depth.

sitions at several settings to get the best results and compare the individual compositions for research and reference to be used the next time you want to picture the same kind of subject.

The double exposure can be used creatively to combine two pictures of one person, two persons in one picture, two angles of a single scene, two scenes in one composition, or three or more images, as in a photographic composition in the school of Duchamp's painting *Nude*

93. A zoom lens on the Nikon S was moved during the exposure to produce this composition in multi-image.

94. The 35mm is an ideal camera for taking informal shots of a wedding. The intensity of the activity demands that the photographer work quickly. There are many unusual and striking angles possible to eliminate the tired old clichés of wedding photography.

95. Screen wire was used over the lens to create the star effect. For this kind of picture, exposure must be made for the strength of the light.

Descending a Staircase. Djon Mili has done exciting things using this technique with electronic flash.

Finally, a technique that is a gimmick, but which can be useful, is the placing of a mirror on the front of the lens to reflect the picture being taken. A prism can be used in much the same fashion. Two or more detailed images may be formed by putting the mirrors against the lens. The two or more images will be projected to the film with none of the problems that confront the photographer when he is shooting into mirrors.

If one picture is worth a thousand words, isn't it possible that several picture compositions combined into one composition will create a picture worth proportionately more words? The multi-image techniques are for a special purpose and perhaps gimmicky devices of composition, but if the picture contains its message, the end justifies the means regardless of the philosophy of purist versus non-purist photographer.

SCREEN THE SCENE

If you are looking for a fresh method of presenting a much photographed scene, a piece of wire screen might be the answer. Cut the household wire screen to fit the adapter ring that fits over your lens. There is no appreciable alteration in the exposure when using one piece of wire. As you shoot directly into the light source (the sun, street lamps, etc.), the wire grid causes a breaking of the light rays which creates a refraction of the light and produces a star effect. One layer of wire produces a four-sided star. Two pieces of wire placed over each other will produce an eight-sided or pointed star. There is a one-stop increase in exposure when using two pieces of wire. Fluted glass may also create a comparable effect.

If your 35mm is a barrel focus, the position of the star effect will change as the barrel is rotated. With a rangefinder viewer, the results are unseen until the film is processed. With a reflex housing or prism viewer, the effect may be studied before shooting the scene. The best results will be had when using the medium and telephoto lenses. Not that excellent and dramatic images cannot be made with a wide-angle or normal length lens. They can. Occasionally a stripe pattern will be recorded on the film because the wire will be at the right distance to be "seen" by the lens. Telephoto lenses have a length and point of focus that make it nearly impossible for the wire image to show. Even with the lens stopped down to the smallest opening, as will be the case when shooting directly into the sun, the wire shape will not be recorded.

In daylight, exposures will be at optimum. Because of the brightness of light emanating from shooting directly into the sun, you should use a film that is not overly fast. A medium-fast or medium-slow film is best. The fine grain slow films are also good because they have extremely slow ASA indexes. Unless you are going to alter the development of the fast-type films to reduce the speed, or you expect to use filters on the fast films, do not use them. You will have undesirable over-exposure which will prove impossible to print to maximum tonality.

With medium-fast films, your exposure range will be from 1/500 at f:32, to 1/1000 at f:22, without a filter. Should you use a red, yellow, or orange filter, the film

96. When shooting into screen wire and into the sun, there is the possibility of getting a greater range of tone and detail in the picture if the light source is weaker.

97. A red filter and screen wire were used in making this picture. The sun reflecting in the puddle forms another star.

speed will be reduced in proportion to the filter factor. Yellow has a factor of 2, red has a factor of 7, and orange has a factor of 3. The filter factor will be divided into the film speed or ASA to determine the adjusted ASA for your meter. The wire, when added with the filter, will adjust the exposure further if more than one piece is used together. A single thickness of wire requires no compensation in exposure.

Because you are shooting into the sun, there will be a composition in silhouette.

The degree of silhouetted form will depend on the intensity of the light source. The illustration of the sculpture with the cross-like sun burst has a high degree of detail for a backlighted subject. The early morning sun with which this was lighted has less intensity than later in the day. If you understand the tonal reduction to strong bold blacks and whites with delicate grays tying the composition together, you can successfully use silhouetting to great advantage.

98. Vaseline rubbed on a pane of glass with a small clear opening left in the center was used to create this misty composition. Focus was on the kids, and the smear of vaseline caused the surroundings to lose sharpness

GREASED GLASS

In addition to the use of screen wire or fluted glass, there are other devices that can create unusual effects in your pictures. You might try using in front of the lens a piece of clear glass which has been smeared with vaseline on the edges. If the center is kept clean and the edges coated, the effect will be a streaking of the image construction and the subject will appear in great motion. The perimeter will be less

sharp than the uncoated center area. You might also use a piece of wadded wax paper to give a refracting surface. This will work best if a hole is torn in the center to allow a sharp image to record in combination with the soft diffused image which will appear through the waxed surface. Cellophane may be used to achieve the same effect. However, if you are working in color, you can obtain even more startling effects by using colored cellophane. There will be a sharp, full-fidelity image

99. Humor is the one area of photography that few photographers will attempt. For some reason the camera is considered to be for serious use only, and seldom are funny or humorous pictures taken.

in one area of the picture, and the rest of the composition will be soft with a monotone of color.

One other device that might be used for a departure from the usual image is the fitting of a mirror to the lens which will cause a reflection of the picture being photographed. By placing a mirror at approximately half the diameter of the lens, there will be a sharply reflected image of the true image that will produce an effect similar to water on a street. This may be used very effectively with outdoor scenes or with pictures of people.

HUMOR

The area most void in the medium of photography is the subject of humor. There has never been an adaptation of the cartoon, satire, or joke-type humor to the photographic process. Not that the camera is incapable of recording laughable situations, but that photographers have never adapted themselves to using the camera for photographing the amusing events of life. The devotion to the documentation of man's misfortunes or the beauty of nature has dominated the creative interests of photographers since the medium began. Only in the 1950's did anyone think in terms of humor as seen by the camera. Elliott Erwitt assembled a very interesting exhibition of his fun-poking and satirical pictures. Jerry Yulsman undertook to create a "keystone cop"

kind of satire with his camera. Others were toying with the idea of the camera as a recorder of comedy or humor.

While the picture of the camera in the field of humor may seem very dark, the situation is not altogether black. Not every photographer is going to have the capacity to enjoy the humorous situations around him, but almost everyone will occasionally see something funny to photograph. Just as few people can tell a funny joke with the punch line falling properly into place, so few photographers can tell a funny story in their pictures. On occasion, however, the event is ready-made and the photographer has only to recognize the humor. For this, the greatest asset the photographer can have is his sense of humor.

The 35mm photographer is better equipped to see and record humorous actions than his big camera colleagues. Since most humorous situations occur quickly and last only seconds, 35mm techniques are perhaps the only methods useable for successfully capturing the fleeting action.

Creativity is thought by most people to mean that intangible characteristic of seriousness. Whether applied to nature or people, seriousness of intent seems to guide the thinking of the dedicated mind concerned with the creative aspects of his art medium. Photography is no exception. And when one ventures into the realm of humor, the product is thought to be on a no higher art level than the cartoon is considered by fine artists. I could not disagree more completely. Photographic humor requires the same discipline of techniques to select and record as serious pictures. And, more important, humorous pictures require the viewer to have the capacity to appreciate the photographer's humor.

HISTORICAL DOCUMENTATION

The most graphic report the twentieth century has of the great Civil War conflicts is the documentation in photographs produced by Mathew Brady and other contemporary photographers. Theirs was the initial photojournalistic effort and is a most valuable record today. Since that first war coverage, the camera has been carried into combat by some of the most illustrious photographers of all time. In World War II, great pictures were made by great photographers. W. Eugene Smith, Carl Mydans, and Robert Capa are only three who gained their place in photography because of their sensitive pictures of the devastation of war. David Douglas Duncan, Mike Rougier, Max Desfor and many others continued this tradition of great photography under the handicap of battle conditions. Their pictures are vivid reminders of "how-it-was." These photographers shared the lives of the soldiers and shared their experiences with the world, through their pictures. The camera recorded for history the full and horrible effects of war. Can any word documentarian say as much in as little space?

The 35mm camera has been the combat companion of all the great twentieth century war photographers. Because of its handiness of operation, speed of use, and quantity of film-per-roll, the 35mm offers more convenience to the men who have to concern themeslves with staying alive

while making their pictures. Creative? I doubt that any of the photographers who dug their faces into the mud of Korea, the beaches of Normandy, or the rocks of Corregidor were concerned with the "art for art's sake" theory of photography. Yet each of the men mentioned plus scores of others were capable of producing finely composed pictures. Why? Because they knew their equipment and employed its full potential. It was said of David Duncan's Korean War[1] coverage, that the pictures were as beautifully designed as if he had all day in which to select the composition. His vision plus the application of his 35mm camera techniques combined to create living images of dying fighting men.

Not all human misery was to be found in the jungles of unnamed islands. The Farm Security Administration proved this. A talented corp of photographers under the direction of Roy Stryker presented the problems of migrant and destitute people in pictures with a power impossible with words. The 35mm camera traveled with the Model T Fords from Oklahoma to California. The small camera enabled the photographer to get close to the people without causing them to shrink away with objections, or resentment to showing their plight. The gigantic project of FSA was responsible for much of the technique of photojournalism as practiced today. And many of the great men of photojournalism are the pioneers of Stryker's tutoring. Gordon Parks, Arthur Rothstein, Dorothea Lange, and Carl Mydans all participated in the FSA projects.

Television films will perhaps become the official files of historical facts, because of the medium's tremendous coverage. But,

[1] *This Is War*, David Douglas Duncan (Harper and Brothers)

the efforts of the 35mm still-cameraman long ago set the stage and developed the techniques which the television camera now employs in the documenting of an event. Even if television does reach larger numbers of people, the still picture will never be replaced, for only the stopped, controlled, and created image of a single frame allows the viewer the opportunity to study and read the picture and find all of its meaning. As long as there are people who read William Faulkner, there will be an audience for the still picture. No documentation of people is better undertaken than with the assets afforded the photographer through the 35mm techniques. If the twentieth century is not the best documented century of mankind, it will not be the fault of the photographers. For the equipment of the thirty-five millimeter was born in a century when its services most demanded quick human and mechanical response to a harried universe.

PHOTOJOURNALISM, THE UNIVERSAL LANGUAGE

Photojournalism is the universal language. There are no language barriers in the reading of a picture. In contemporary picture reportage, a French photographer who speaks no other language, may photograph his country's customs, scenery, and people, and make himself understood by most other people in the world. Henri Cartier-Bresson, the world famous French photographer, has spoken eloquently to the world with his camera for the last fifteen years. There is no language barrier for this man or his readers.

The picture as a serious medium of communication in journalism is over two decades old. *Life* and *Look*, both launched in 1936, started the trend toward the maximum use of photographs to tell a story. The product of the work of these two magazines has been the photo essay, or picture story. It is a relatively new adaptation of the very ancient use of pictures to communicate. Early man chiselled crude pictures on the wall of his cave, and the Egyptians used hieroglyphics to tell their story. Today as we read their crude pictures we understand much of the civilization of their people. It is quite possible that in years to come another civilization will read our photographs and learn of our society. And with such 35mm photographers as Cartier-Besson, Robert Capa (about whom it was said, "He was a master of five languages, but his best method of communication was his camera, for he pictured war so all men of all languages could understand"), W. Eugene Smith, Cornell Capa, Ernst Haas, and many others leading the way, photojournalism has become the universal language.

The idea of using pictures (with minimum wordage) to tell a complete story was conceived by the *Time, Inc.*, group. In the late twenties and early thirties, the editors of *Time* and *Fortune* experimented with pictures to present the world's news. Individuals such as Peter Stackpole, Thomas McAvoy (who was the first to use a candid technique to photograph Franklin D. Roosevelt), Margaret Bourke-White, and Alfred Eisenstadt (an ex-button salesman from Germany who had, at the time, created world interest with his 35mm coverage of the Ethiopian War) were the first pioneers of the picture story technique. These four people were the individuals who worked on the experimental publication that resulted in the birth of

Life magazine in November of 1936. Until *Life* began publication, pictures had been used primarily to illustrate textual material. But *Life's* principle was the reverse. For the *Life* format, the pictures would be supplemented by a brief word introduction and captions. And the picture story infant was born.

The picture essay or picture story (I prefer to call a picture group that tells a story completely from beginning to end, an essay), is conceived in the minds of the photographer, writer, researcher, or the magazine editorial staff—or all. A photographer has three major sources to glean his ideas from: one is the newspaper where a short news item about a person, place, or thing suggests picture interpretation. Personal contact with people is another lucrative source of story ideas. And the news events of the day offer picture story ideas. But no matter where the idea comes from, the subject must lend itself to visual treatment. It is one thing to describe a subject in words, but it is something else to photograph the situation. Since a picture story requires visual treatment, the original idea should suggest visual possibilities. Unless it does, no matter how interesting the idea, it will not make a good picture story.

In producing a story, a photographer must follow certain methods of operation so that he will have a complete story. No great importance is placed on equipment. The choice is the photographer's. Contemporary photographers use all cameras from the 35mm to the 8x10 view. The choice is left to the photographer and he usually fits his camera to the style of work he does. There is a predominant use of the 35mm camera because of its portability and ease of handling.

Shooting preparation for the picture story is begun with the basic idea being broken down into a shooting script. Just as the movie cameramen work with a shooting script, so a still cameraman should begin his story in the same manner.

The script is not by any means a rigid schedule. The function of the script is to establish basic ideas and activities. There are many excellent pictures that "just happen" and which no one can predict *will* happen. In the preparation of a script, one should consider that a photo-essay must contain all of the necessary elements that make up a good *written* story. There will be beginning or establishing pictures, a plot or story line, a climax, and a conclusion. If a story is weak on any of these points, the essay will probably be poor.

The pictures must be strong enough to present fully the story with only a few words to introduce the reader to the theme, or to clarify where clarification is needed. As the shooting on the story progresses, the photographer is always aware of a possible "lead" picture. Such a picture contains a powerful impact visually and sums up the story in one composition. The "lead" picture's purpose is to stir the emotion and interest of the reader sufficiently to persuade him to read further. At all times a photojournalist is aware of the maximum emotion or conflict of the subject of the story. The greater the conflict or emotion, the better the pictures will appeal to the reader. A sense of presence in viewing the scene is felt by the reader if the pictures contain these strong qualities. As one is shooting the story, he should explore all of the picture possibilities, for the shooting script in effect is nothing more than just an outline.

100-102. This layout of pictures, part of an extensive study done on an American prison, was used in the *British Photography Magazine,* and was conceived, researched, and designed by the photographer. Although slightly altered from the original, the feeling of the story has been retained. The photojournalist is no longer just a shutter-pusher. Today there must be greater depth and quality of report, and an interpretative point of view. The printed page competes with the television screen. Yet the still picture on the printed page has greater meaning, for it may be viewed and studied as long as the reader wishes. The additional opportunity to study demands more meaningful content in the picture.

VISUAL NOTEMAKING

The technique of journalistic photography which I employ in the production of pictures for many varied publications is not at all unlike the techniques used by writers. The writer will scribble hundreds, even thousands of words and notes to assure himself of complete coverage of the event he is reporting. I do the same thing with a camera. By making a visual note or picture of everything that takes place involving the event or subject, there is seldom any doubt that the story is on film. The editing of the processed film reveals the fullness with which the story was observed and recorded. Very often the studying of the contacts will reveal points or elements of the story that are totally irrelevant to the theme or objective. In my opinion, the presence of such unwanted or unneeded photographs which might distort the point of view of the story teller demands that the photographer have a strong opinion regarding the selection and use of his pictures in context with the original theme as undertaken. Failure to follow through from the visual observation note making, to the editing and selecting of the pictures intended for continuity of story idea, is treading on the very weak premise that someone else might see the story in the same light as the photographer (and perhaps the producer or writer) on the scene.

If the photographer is truly honest with himself and obeys his obligation to his subject, he cannot, and will not allow any editorializing by uninformed or unconcerned persons. To allow even the slightest deviation from the truth as witnessed by the photographer is, in my opinion, a journalistic sin that no amount of confession or penitence-paying can rectify. If the photographer-journalist sees sadistic or villainous characteristics in a subject that the world knows as a sweet-faced, mild mannered being, the photojournalist owes an obligation to himself and his profession to record these observations and present to the uninformed reader the image which is incongruous to the popular image. Failure to hold firm to his journalistic duty of honesty, regardless of editorial objections, is being dishonest with himself and his responsibility to his profession.

A visual statement may be made to have ambiguous meanings by the few selected words placed in association with it. And if a vigilance is not maintained to safeguard against allowing verbal distortions to encroach upon visual truths, the photographer could be guilty of permitting, by omission, the wrong image of the subject to be presented to the reader-viewer. If a wrong statement is made, it is nearly impossible to erase from the mind the impression already made, especially if that impression is one that the reader wanted to have. An excellent point, for example, is the lawyer who manages to inject a terrifically strong statement on behalf of his client into the trial to which the opposition lawyer promptly objects and his objection is sustained by the judge. However, the jury has already heard the statement and human nature makes it impossible to forget the words completely. The combination of words and pictures as a distorted or untrue statement is doubly hard to erase.

My technique of "visual notemaking" is generally practiced by photojournalists in the profession. But, unfortunately, not all photographers follow through to help edit out the pictures which might distort the story or subject. W. Eugene Smith once stated that a misused story is an unused story. I agree, but want to add that correcting a misused story or a mistake in statement, as with erasing words from a jury's mind, is nearly impossible.

One of the reasons so many court judges refuse the admittance of cameras in their courtrooms is their desire to protect the innocent. It is one thing to read the name of an accused rapist in a newspaper and then forget the name, if the man is acquitted. But a visual presentation of the same man and the same story is not easily forgotten, and even if the man is acquitted, he remains convicted in the eyes of many of the people who read and viewed his ordeal. I am not for closed courtrooms. I feel very strongly that a journalist should be allowed the right to report the news honestly as he sees and hears it, whatever his medium. But the photographer has a greater responsibility to his medium to protect himself and his subject from cruel or distorted treatment when his material is placed into someone else's hands.

TOTAL JOURNALISM

The photojournalist is a word and picture man. He must create exciting visual statements and then be able to informatively verify the visual with complementary verbal messages, rendering to the reader the total activity witnessed. The profession of making photographs for the printed page has undergone, and will continue to undergo, exciting, even complex changes. The practice of using the depthless, thin-lined, gimmick picture story is more extinct than the American buffalo. Rapidly replacing the short, nearly meaningless gimmick story that boomed during the 1950's are the in-depth, exhaustive, explorative studies that are pursued with the pictures supported, complemented, dominated, or contrasted by well chosen words. The complete cycle allows the follow-through of the layout to present the image that was created in the mind of the photographer.

There is absolute truth in the theory that no one layout is the only layout. With more or less pages, a story would have to be handled somewhat differently, adding more or less details to the visual. But for the man who conceived and photographed the idea, there is only one image. Too often another mind will distort rather than validate the photographer's filmed image.

I do not advocate that all photographers rise up and make unjust demands of the people who use their pictures. But, I vehemently declare that if photojournalism is to progress, achieve depth and understanding, and survive against other visual competition, photographers must prepare themselves with more than just the ability to expose film. "Total journanlism," which includes the curiosity of a researcher, the questioning of a writer, the reflexes of the photographer, the designing of the art director, and the reader concern of the editor, will be condensed into a working formula that, when activated by the catalyst of a newsworthy subject, will present provocative statements. Occasionally, one picture will sum up the story. More often the complete statement will be made with several pictures juxtapositioned together to form another "picture." The individual photographer who is competent in "total journalism" need never fear that his honesty and integrity will be violated by an unthinking editor. The individual pictures must be strong; the photographer must be capable, enabling the champion statement to solidify in publication.

tion, the 35mm approach will allow the opening up of fresh ways of seeing the same old well-worn photographs usually done of weddings.

WEDDING

Even the routine assignment of photographing a wedding for a friend or for professional purposes can be treated with story-telling interest by relying on the techniques allied with the 35mm camera. The need for the extra light of a flash is eliminated even while working in the usually dimly lighted church. Most ministers do not like having pictures made in the church because of the distraction of the flash. The taking of one picture can interrupt the ceremony and shatter an atmosphere of religious seriousness. But with the combination of fast film, fast lenses, and available light, realistic documents of the marriage vows may be made without distraction.

In place of the single picture, several pictures may be made which, when printed and placed in the wedding album, would be a movie strip series. The opportunities to get pictures that are not in the cliched category of antiquated wedding photography will increase with the application of 35mm photography. From the formal portraits of the bride, to the newlyweds' departure on their honeymoon, the 35mm camera techniques can accomplish quality with greater coverage. Not only does the bride get a more intimate record of this most important day in her life, but she also gets a greater choice of pictures. The usual pictures of a wedding will be made easier, and in addi-

THE SHIFT IN INDUSTRY

Today nothing is thought of a photographer's entering an industrial plant to take pictures only with a 35mm camera. But it has not always been accepted that a fully qualified professional of industrial photography could use a miniature camera. The view camera and industry were synonymous, and the pictures were stereotyped. Of course, there was an exception or two where the big camera user managed, by his unusual talent, to ascend to creative heights not usually possible with the inhibiting disadvantages of view-camera techniques.

But, as the restlessness of the photographers who had devoted themselves to industrial photography grew, and as new faces appeared who were not in agreement that the view camera and industry were synonymous, the smaller cameras gained a place in the big world of business. Here the 35mm qualified itself as a permanent part of the creative photographer's equipment by the broader scope of coverage permitted and the quality of the images possible. As a few photographers employed the 35mm camera in their work and produced pictures that were less stereotyped and more spontaneous, other photographers began concurring by producing increasingly interesting, "less stiff" industrial photographs. The acceptance of the 35mm format had broken through the "four minute mile" barrier. Today every

103 -104.   These two shots of a DeLaval separator and a plant control box, both made on location, are two examples of how quality 35mm photography is making the industrial photographer's job easier. Both of these pictures were made without the restrictions of the huge camera and tripod used by industrial photographers of a decade ago.

105. Control Methods Plant, 1961. The 135mm lens was used to compress the product and the workers into one composition. Available light was used.

106. The bellows permitted moving in for this close-up, a measurement of a Boice Gauge. Natural light was used.

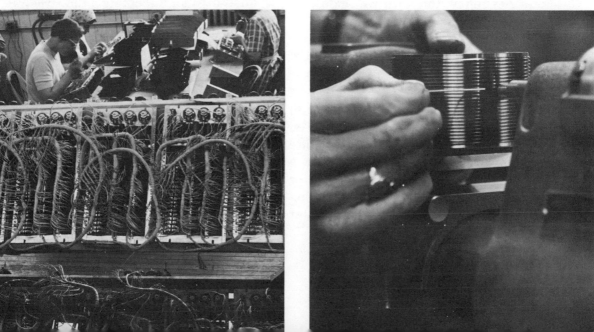

creative talent of industrial photography employs the versatility of the 35mm camera to enhance his interpretation of a jungle of pipes and stones.

I remember the first time that I carried a *Leica* into an industrial plant. The man with whom I was to work asked if I intended to shoot some color slides. His question was usual, for the 35mm was used only to shoot color, in his opinion. I replied by saying that I expected to shoot much of the black and white with the *Leica,* and that I did not intend to shoot any color. He reacted with a typically doubting expression, but I think he was tolerant of my youth. As we toured the massive structures, I quickly pictured anything and everything that appealed to me. I shot eight rolls of film that morning, and as far as I know did not shoot any of the usual scenes that most other photographers had pictured. My pictures caused a few double takes when they were presented, for in them I had recorded the personality of the plant and not the superstructures. I have had a long and fruitful association with this company and the 35mm camera is a commonplace piece of equipment now.

What does the 35mm camera with its accessories offer the creative industrial photographer? To answer this question it would be well to compare the pictures possible with 35mm techniques as compared to the techniques of the larger formats.

The advantage of a freer movement in working is by far the greatest asset. The 35mm camera enables the photographer to set his camera for out-of-doors at a nominal shutter speed of about 125th or 250th of a second with a corresponding lens opening and be able to stop almost any action he sees. He could employ the hyperfocal principle of pre-setting the lens for focus and sharpness and shoot without fear of unsharp areas. The normal 50mm lens is generally enough to cover most subjects, but on occasions in tight quarters where space is lacking, the wide angle lens is needed. This too can be hand-held where the larger cameras demand a tripod. In many cases, the space is too restricted to get the tripod in the area.

Of course, there will always be the continuing argument about correction of vertical lines. This lack of correcting features which are possible in view cameras is often a disadvantage with the 35mm camera. But is it not better to get a picture with the verticals slightly tilted than to miss the composition altogether? If you use the 35mm camera knowing that the verticals are going to be less than straight, you compensate for them by the angle of shooting. Dramatic accentuation may be created by selecting an angle where the lines, by their tilting, cause a stronger design and eye appeal. This is employing a disadvantage to a creative advantage. And, if there is a need to have the verticals as straight as possible, there are ways to help keep them straight.

First, if you are shooting a tall structure, the easiest means of keeping the lines straight is to elevate yourself to an angle that permits looking down as well as looking up. For example, if you are shooting a superstructure in a refinery, you need the perspective and distortion at a minimum; you would climb a nearby structure which would be high enough to allow the lens to see up and down when pointed at the center of the structure. Additional correction could be made by tilting the easel in enlargement. If an additional

107. More extensive industrial coverage without work stoppage is easily accomplished with 35mm photography. Because of the high level of light necessary to the conduct of plant work, any lens from wide-angle to telephoto may be used without supplementary light sources. This photograph was taken with a 35mm wide-angle shooting at f:8, employing the hyperfocal focusing to maintain optimum sharpness.

structure is not nearby, you can get moderate correction by using a tall ladder. A ladder can be used effectively when taking pictures with the 35mm, because the camera can be hand-held.

But we are considering primarily the creative applications of the 35mm format in the field of industrial photography. And because the 35mm techniques offer approaches not possible with the bigger cameras, we should concern ourselves with how to apply the techniques to produce pictures taking advantage of these methods. If we are going to duplicate that which is possible with the bigger cameras, why use thirty-five millimeter?

Perhaps the most significant feature of the techniques of 35mm photography when applied to industry, architecture, or advertising, is mobility. Combine mobility with an interchangeable lens feature, and you have a team that challenges the creative photographer to his full capacity. With a single camera around your neck, and two or three different length lenses handy, there is a creative range as wide as sight itself.

We have mentioned angles of shooting as applied to industry. The same thinking would be applied in the search for new and exciting ways of photographing buildings. Architects are concerned with the

108. The 35mm in industry is becoming widely accepted because of the greater ease of work it permits and the different types of pictures possible with more mobile equipment. This shot at the Ethyl Corporation in Baton Rouge, Louisiana, was spontaneously made while walking through the plant.

three dimensional qualities of the buildings they design. Unless the photographs can dramatically demonstrate the depth of the building, the pictures are usually only records of a project. But, if the photographer visually interprets the design of the building in three dimensional terms, the photographs become important as the statement of the intentions of the architects. In my own experience, using a wide-angle lens and shooting hand-held at angles and positions which would be otherwise impossible, I have created graphic documentations of the architect's original concepts. When you work indoors, it is not too often that increased illumination is required to record the designs of the interiors. Sometimes it might require that a tripod be used to enable a time exposure of a few seconds, but this time exposure is considerably shorter than would be demanded by larger equipment.

Architectural and industrial photography are newcomers to the 35mm world of photography. Progress has been good because the photographers who would not be inhibited by traditions have proved the merits of the "hand camera" by the exciting and high quality pictures that they have produced. The pictures were not made by repeating the images of the big camera technique and by the mathematical or numerical terms of f:stops and lens openings. The photographs were the products of the inventive and creative imagination of the photographer who was willing to abandon all accepted practices to speak for himself. His visual voice has been strong enough so that many art directors and public relations men are asking for the 35mm approach. Unfortunately, many men not talented in the techniques of the 35mm are using it, but in the same manner as their view camera. I have seen pictures produced with the 35mm that look exactly like the image of an 8x10 view, because the same approach and style has been used as would have been used with the view camera. None of the spontaneous swiftness in recording the personality of the plant is present. The photographer is misusing the 35mm as a creative image maker.

ADVERTISING

Editorial advertising is a term that was invented in the late 1950's. Its meaning is: "pictures that are photojournalistic and story telling." Today's magazines are full of them. Even the rigidly posed photographs are aimed at informal, editorial-type images. The 35mm photographer is responsible for this concept in advertising.

Ed Henderson, who was an "ad exec" handling the *New York Equitable Life* account, originated a series of ads built around a single picture spread over two pages for dramatic impact. He sought out pictures that had strong stopping power. Most of the pictures he selected were pictures by photojournalists who worked with the 35mm camera. The advertising campaign was a tremendous success. Most significant was the acceptance of the 35mm pictures in the large camera kingdom. A revolution and dethronement had begun. The 35mm camera had come out of its case to start an exciting change in the visual traditions of advertising.

Just taking a series of pictures with the 35mm camera does not make your pictures better. Employing the mechanical methods of lenses, films, shooting angles, and other devices of the medium are the factors which create images individual to the 35mm format.

The pictures which you see here are from an advertising campaign undertaken by a conventional banking institution. The "ad exec's" only direction to me was to find the *personality* of the bank. For many hours I looked, walked about, and photographed the activities of a day at the bank. None of the pictures was intended to glamourize either the bank or the people. I used wide-angle lenses, available light, telephoto lenses, and design, plus my own curiosity to explore the inner workings of the firm.

Some four hundred pictures were taken. The advertisements became a visual introduction to the humanistic qualities of an intangible institutional business. These pictures are the product of my thoughts at the time of the shooting. Were I to go back and do the assignment over, in all probability the pictures would be different. The creative values are perhaps partly due to the lack of knowledge of the function of the business. More knowledge of the bank would influence the pictures that would be taken. Unfamiliarity can be both an advantage and a disadvantage. The disadvantage is ignorance of the validity of statements being made by the selection of the compositions. Lack of knowledge could cause untrue or distorted pictures. And in advertising, anything that is misleading must be avoided.

There are no specific formulas by which you can approach the near virgin fields of advertising, architecture, and industrial 35mm photography. The applications of the techniques as I have outlined them in other parts of this book, the curiosity you will have for the subject, and the exploration of your imagination will determine the quality of the pictures you will take. The challenge is yours. The fulfillment and meeting of that challenge will be the reward.

TECHNIQUES THAT HELP

I. Panning and Motion

In still photography there is often the need to accentuate the feeling of motion or to pinpoint a subject within a framework of movement. The technique of "panning," or following the subject, shooting, and following through, is used to achieve both of these results. The method is simple, but excitingly strong pictures may be made by using it.

The selection of a shutter speed is of first concern for the photographer when panning is to be used. A speed which will allow some measure of stopping the slower movements of the subject, and which at the same time will allow all other motion to blur, should be used. When the panning is done, the movement of the subject is followed from a point in advance of the time or place when the shutter is tripped. Care should be taken to match the speed of the subject to the speed of the panning. Coordination of timing of both is important. A lot of action can be stopped just by gearing the ratio of panning to movement of subject. For example, with a running subject moving left to right, a 1/25th setting will stop much action. But you will have to get the feel of following with the camera the subject in tempo with the speed of the subject.

As the subject approaches, you pre-focus at a point directly in front of you. When

109. Industrial companies and corporations are producing more and more magazines for employee and outside distribution. This picture, taken with a 50mm and a single-lens reflex, was done for the *New York Telephone Review Magazine*.

110. Industrial annual reports of facts and figures are being dressed up with highlights of the yearly operation. Pictures that show an organization's activities are used in layouts that present visual evidence of the company's success. This picture of a county fair was used by the Central Hudson Gas Company in their annual report.

111. The biggest boom in photography to present a message has been in advertising. Big companies and corporations have turned to the editorial picture to sell their products. Insurance and soft-drink companies and banks have switched from the old stereotyped pictures, and the national influence has extended to local firms. This group of pictures and advertisements is from a campaign for the Ulster County Savings Bank of Kingston, New York. Every professional photographer has the opportunity to introduce this type of advertising in his own locale.

112. Ulster County Savings Bank, 1962. This is only one of scores of pictures used in a "banking in action" advertising campaign. All of the pictures were taken in or around the bank. No posing or staging of pictures was attempted; as things happened, they were photographed.

the subject reaches that point, you, having had the subject in your viewfinder leading to that point, trip the shutter, and *keep* following the movement beyond the point where the focus was made. The camera is being moved in tempo with the subject and the shutter is open for the exposure at a point directly in front of you. The subject will be in sharp focus, to a degree, and the rest of the composition will be fuzzy, but recognizable. The faster the subject moves, the faster the shutter speed you can use. Conversely, the slower moving the subject, the slower will be the requirement of the shutter speed. But, perhaps the most important element is getting the twist of the movement with the camera in tempo with the speed of the subject. Study the pictures to see how the movement of the camera matches the movement of the subject. Practice is needed with this technique, but once it is handled correctly, it becomes a very useful device.

The opposite of panning is the technique of letting the camera remain stationary while the picture composition moves. For this the shutter speed is also important, for the speed must be slow enough to allow the motion to show, but at the same time be fast enough to hand-hold safely. For speeding objects such as racing cars, horses, or the like, no problem prevails. But, if the tempo of the subject is no faster than a walk, the shutter speed will have to be very slow, and hand-holding the camera could spoil the results. A tripod might be needed. Here again, a bit of practice will let you know the degree of safety or ability you have with holding slow speeds.

II. Compositional Devices

There are several devices of composition

113. Wright Adams House, 1955. The 35mm is also capable of doing quality pictures in the field of architecture. Unfortunately, too few photographers who specialize in architectural subjects are willing to attempt the fresh approach possible with the hand-held 35mm and a wide-angle lens.

which the 35mm photographer should recognize and use. Not that these are to be exclusive with the 35mm camera user, but rather the small camera is more suitable to the uses of these devices.

A. Foreground Objects

Because the 35mm lenses have a much greater depth of field than even the big

114-116. These are three examples of "panning." The photographer tracks the subject, shoots when the subject is in front of the camera, and follows through. The subject is in sharp focus but the foreground and background are blurred.

brother 2¼ square formats, the use of objects in the foreground is easier to employ in creating a feeling of depth through the establishing of a foreground plane which complements the overall design of the photograph. The objects in the foreground may be sharp and a definite part of the composition, or they may be out of focus with only partial meaning within the picture.

In some cases, the foreground design is an unidentifiable object which is being looked through to frame the subject. But regardless of the compositional meaning of the foreground, the use of it will make the viewer more aware of the subject of the picture.

B. Perspective

Again, the greater depth possible because of the shorter length 35mm lenses makes the use of perspective in compositions a natural technique for the creative 35mm photographer. There are two kinds of perspective.

One is *forced perspective* which directs one's viewing or eye-travel with a commanding strength. The second is the *receding perspective* which employs the diminishing shape and size of objects to create the illusion of depth. To define the two applications of perspective further, let us discuss them individually.

First, the forced perspective is one which usually circumnavigates the central subject. You cannot visually get to the subject without encountering the design surrounding the subject. Most often forced perspective is achieved with the establishing of an extremely strong foreground. But unlike the foreground framing, the perspective is achieved with the establishing of an extremely strong foreground. And unlike the foreground framing, the perspective use of the foreground employs

117. The opposite of panning is to hold the camera still and let the subjects move. The central figure in the striped shirt was wanted in focus, while the activity of the room as the students departed was to be blurred. A fifteenth of a second accomplished both.

the size relationships of the objects in the composition as a part of the photograph's design.

The receding perspective is perhaps the easiest form of design for creating the illusion of depth in a two dimensional composition. With this method, there is a repetition and diminishing of size of the same object. A picket fence is a good example. If you stand close to a picket fence and look down the fence to the other end, the immediate pickets will be large and fill your view. The pickets get smaller as the fence moves to the end. The last picket is very small when compared to the nearest picket, yet both are actually the same size. The feeling of depth is created by comparing the nearest picket to the farthest picket. Of course, the application of the repeating, receding perspective is not limited to fences or inanimate objects. Marching soldiers, lined-up equipment, stacked building materials, or any other subject can be handled effectively with this device of composition.

III. Selective Focus

The eye sees that which the mind selects for viewing. The lens sees that which the mind wants seen. And the control of the focus of the lens will assist the transferring of the photographer's viewing to the viewing enjoyed by the observer of his picture. The technique which is of great assistance to the photographer for pinpointing vision is selective focus. With this method of concentrated viewing, the lens is usually used at a large aperture or f:stop. The larger the lens opening, the less sharpness will appear in the picture. By focusing on the one important object in the composition, all else is reduced to unimportant space fillers, and the total concentration is on the central subject of the picture.

One characteristic of selective focus is the formation of circular shapes of out-of-focus highlight areas. This is called *circle of confusion*. When a highlight is made to be completely out of focus, the bright image forms a circle. Users of single lens reflex 35mm cameras can see this happening as they select the point of focus. Whether the highlights are artificial light or sunlight, the effect is the same. If you are taking a picture under a tree and shooting upward into the light filtering through the leaves, you may put the leaves completely out of focus, and circles of highlights will be created. Combining the many halo-like circles with a pretty face makes an angelic composition of a pretty girl. The most effective application of selective focus is achieved when all viewing is concentrated on the subject.

IV. Depth of Field

Perhaps the most misunderstood but most useful device of control a photographer has is the depth of field. Proper application of the depth of field technique can be of significant meaning in a photographic composition. What is meant by depth of field? The term is applied to the total area of sharpness of a given f:stop when focused at a given point. For example, if the lens is focused at fifteen feet, and an f:stop of f:11 is being used, by looking at the depth of field scale on the camera, you would see that the total area of sharpness is from nine feet (the nearest point) to forty-five feet (the farthest point), with the critical focus being at fifteen feet. Everything that falls within this 35-foot range will be recorded sharply.

119. The depth of field is the maximum area of sharpness covered when the lens is set at a given f:stop. This shot of buggies was made at f:16 with the 50mm lens focused at fifteen feet.

118. In this example of selective focus, the point of focus is on the young boy. The area of sharpness was restricted by keeping the lens at a big f:stop. The fuzzy shapes suggest their identity without having importance equal to that of the boy.

By studying the depth of field scale, you can see which f:stop is required to produce the range of sharpness the picture demands. For instance, if a composition with a foreground object eight feet away and a big scenic background which reaches to infinity is to be made, you could see that when the lens is focused at fifteen feet and f:16, this range of sharpness would be allowed. You would set f:16 on the lens and a shutter speed to match according to the light present. Also, if you had a central subject which was four feet away and you wanted it sharp, but at the same time you wanted as much depth as possible, you could turn the focus scale until it lined up four feet opposite the smallest lens opening. The critical focus would line up with the focus index and the farthest point of sharpness would line up opposite the far side of the depth of field scale indicating the range of sharpness. There would be no need to focus on any one object, because the depth of field is taking care of everything from four feet to the maximum point of the depth of the lens.

As you plan to use the depth of field, get the camera out and study the scale with relationship to the f:stop and focus. And remember, that the depth of field scale will change with every length lens. For example, a 35mm wide-angle lens will have a greater depth of field at f:5.6 than a 50mm lens; a 50mm will have a greater depth than a 135mm lens, etc. To use the depth of field effectively and creatively for sharp or limited focus, check each lens as you use it.

V. Hyperfocal Distance

A technique which is akin to the depth of field, or rather employs the depth of

120. Maximum sharpness from the trellis to the house is possible because of depth of field, which insures a forced perspective.

field, is the hyperfocal distance. With this method of shooting you can pre-set your camera so as to function without need of focusing each time a picture is made. And you can get the absolute maximum sharpness. In fact, when the hyperfocal distance technique is used, you are turning the camera into a fixed focus principle such as the box camera. With this operation you take a meter reading to determine the lens and shutter combination needed for the light available. The f:stop is lined up *on the depth of field scale* opposite the infinity index. This is the farthest point which will be in focus. The nearest point of focus will be the footage that will be lined up opposite the same f:stop on the *near side of the focus scale*. The critical point of focus will be opposite the index for focus. For example, with a 50mm lens when the exposure is to be 1/250 at f:16, you would place the f:16 on the depth of field scale (not the actual lens opening) opposite the infinity index on the focus scale. This is the farthest point of sharpness. The nearest point of sharpness is eight feet as indicated by the f:16 on depth of field on the near side of the focus scale. The critical point of focus is fifteen feet. As long as you stay eight feet from a subject, you can shoot everything in sight and have sharp images without focusing the camera for each picture. The coverage of sharpness will vary as the lens length varies (see chart), but here again, if you become familiar with the characteristics of the lens, you will soon know the range of sharpness or non-sharpness the lens will produce when set at the hyperfocal distance.

122. The depth of field scale of a 50mm lens is read by checking the f:stop at each side of the point of focus. The distances from the closest to the farthest points, which are opposite the f:stop employed for the exposure, indicate the range of depth and sharpness.

121. The four most useable lens-lengths for hyperfocal technique.

LENS	f: stops									
	1.5 F-C	2 F-C	3.5 F-C	4 F-C	5.6 F-C	8 F-C	11 F-C	16 F-C	22 F-C	32 F-C
35mm			35-18	30-16	20-12	15-7.5	11-5.5	7.5-3.8	5.5-2	
50mm	200-100	100-50		75-35	50-25	30-18	24-12	17-8.5	12-6	8-4
90mm				70-35	40-20	50-20	20-12	15-7	12-5.5	7.5-3.8
135mm				200-150	290-145	165-110	150-85	110-60	80-40	55-27

F is the point of focus which lines up when infinity is opposite the f: stop

C is the closest or nearest footage of sharpness which aligns with the f: stop on the depth of field scale

123. The hyperfocal distance principle, as illustrated with the 50mm (two-inch) lens:
To find the hyperfocal distance, place the selected f:stop of the depth of field scale opposite the infinity mark on the focus scale. This will automatically line up eight feet on the near or close side of the focus scale with the f:stop. The focus index will indicate the critical point of focus. In the above illustration, f:16 has been chosen for the exposure. Infinity is placed opposite f:16 on the depth of field scale. This lines up eight feet opposite f:16 on the near side of the focus, while the focus index shows fifteen feet as the critical point of focus. The camera may now be used as a fixed-focus instrument. No focusing is necessary as long as the range of shooting distance is within the eight feet to infinity range. The hyperfocal technique is an excellent one for shooting parades, sporting events, and other out-of-doors activities.

VI. *Nighttime*

While not a technique as with the depth of field or selective focus, the photography of nighttime is an approach to photography that offers some exciting pictures. In my book, *Night Photography* (Chilton, Philadelphia), the many techniques of successful photography at night are described in detail. The 35mm photographer has an added advantage which makes the night more attractive. Because of fast lenses and fast films available, the burden of bulky equipment and long exposures is completely eliminated. In fact, there are very few situations where an exposure meter can not be used to calculate the required lens and shutter settings. Instantaneous shooting at night is just as possible as in daylight. Of course, all of the principles of daylight shooting (composition, panning, selective focus, etc.) are to be employed as creatively as possible. Just because there is a minimum of light does not mean you abandon the devices of design. For the absence of light will oftentimes aid in accentuating the subject being photographed. Dramatic lighting effects are ever present for recognition and use. You should take full advantage of light, or the absence of it, to record your impressions or interpretations. The cloak of darkness can be opened up to reveal a bright new world of discovery.

124. Mallet, Louisiana, 1955. This is an example of how a picture can be taken with hyperfocal distance. The camera was set at f:16 for one-fiftieth of a second. By setting f:16 on the depth of field scale opposite to the infinity index on the focus scale, the point of focus fell on fifteen feet, with the nearest point of the depth of field being opposite the ten-foot position. This picture was made without focusing because everything from ten feet to infinity was in sharp focus and position.

PART IV

Creativity Extends to the Darkroom

Anyone who thinks that the creative process is concluded at the moment of exposure is not aware of the full cycle of the photographic medium. Such thinking might be prompted by laziness, demands of time, or lack of knowledge of the controls possible in the darkroom. Assuming the latter factor is more true than the first two, we will try to outline some of the methods that can be contributed to the darkroom part of the creative cycle.

FILM DEVELOPING

For the greater majority of the time, the processing of 35mm film will be handled carefully and cleanly with no alteration in the routine of procedure. We will not devote space to the elementary processing of 35mm, for anyone who has not progressed past this stage is not photographically mature enough to cope with the controls we are going to discuss. If you think you are incompetent in processing, get a manual on basic processing, and, perhaps with the aid of a friend, learn the ritual of rolling the film on the spool and follow the directions for conventional processing. Only then will the controls of film developing be of any meaning to you.

Because the 35mm photographer ventures into regions that test the materials as well as the photographer, it is not uncommon that a film has been exposed beyond its functional range, and great compensations in the developing are required. Do not be afraid to try anything once. I once shot a roll of Plux X film at an ASA 4000, which in theory meant that I was wasting my time. But by developing the film in D-23 at ninety-four degrees for thirty-five minutes, I got printable negatives and exciting pictures. Of course when you border on disaster, as happens when very high temperatures are used for developing film, you must do additional work.

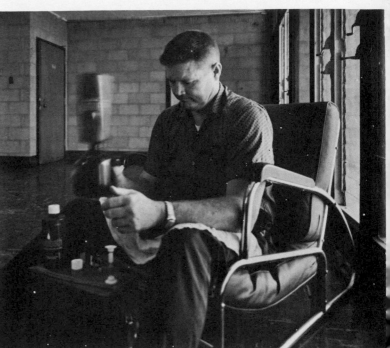

125 -127. These pictures demonstrating the Unibath process were taken on location in a prison. Progress in on-the-spot processing is being made and will enable photographers to follow their work more closely.

128. Mrs. Vincent Astor, Rhinebeck, New York. By rating the film at 4000 and developing to infinity, this picture was made under severely adverse lighting conditions. The increased grain enhances the feeling of the situation. Darkroom maneuvers can often save pictures that would be lost otherwise.

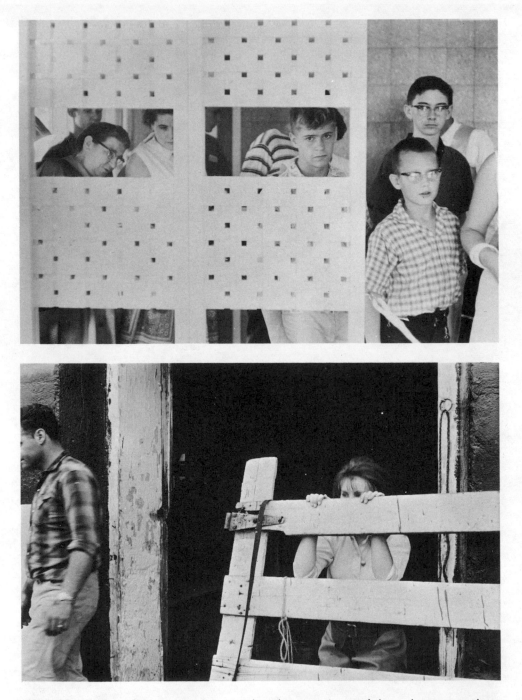

129 -130. When making prints, be sure that the negative and the enlarger are clean and that all equipment is functioning properly. One should realize that the print is the product of the photographic process which will be viewed by the audience. Good print quality is a prerequisite of good photography.

For example, all of the other chemicals must be heated to the approximate temperatures. It is advisable to reduce gradually the height of the temperature in each succeeding solution. And you must add the potassium chrome alum solution to the procedure. Here is how it would work:

D-23

Water	....	24 ounces
Elon	....	1/4 ounce
Sodium Sulfite....	3 ounces	145 grains
Water to make	....	32 ounces

Heat to maximum temperature
Exposed at . . .

ASA 160 (normal)	...........70° @	12 minutes
ASA 400	...........................80°	12
ASA 800	...........................80°	22
ASA 2000	...........................85°	24

These are daylight combinations. Artificial light will be at half ASA. Second solution is potassium chrome alum in lieu of acetic acid. The temperature should be several degrees less than the developer, but still very warm. Three minutes in this solution is sufficient.

Hypo is also warmer than usual, but less than the alum. Fresh hypo should always be used when forcing film in hot solutions. The extra hardening of the alum is further strengthened by the use of fresh hypo.

The wash should begin at a temperature slightly less than the hypo and gradually be reduced to about seventy-five degrees. A wetting agent such as *Photo-flo* will assist the film in drying.

Note: The greatest danger that will prevail when developing at high temperatures is the suddenness of temperature change. For example, when the film is in the hot developer, the gelatine expands. If the film is dunked into a cold potassium alum hardener, the film will harden while the emulsion is still expanded and the images separated. Reticulation will occur and possibly ruin the pictures. The shock of hot to cold chemicals is similar to your reaction to cold water after taking a hot shower. Of course, extra care is required in the handling of negatives processed in hot solutions. And *never* wipe the film surface with a squeegee or sponge. Let the film dry without touching the soft surfaces.

Using heated chemicals is not a technique you will employ creatively every day, but if the situation demands drastic action, do not hinder your creative range by the restrictions of conventional processing. The developer D-23 has been used as an illustration, but it is by no means the only recommended chemical. Here is a list of other excellent developers for this kind of application.

Developers	Degrees			
	70°	75°	80°	85°
X-500	10 min.	7.5	5	3
Acufine	5	3.5	2.5	2
UFG	4	2.5	2	
D-76	12	9	6	4.5
Dektol (1-2)	4	3	2	

The advent of the monochemicals for film processing has helped extend the darkroom's contribution to creativity. *Unibath*[1] with its one step processing procedure has opened up new thinking about film processing. On the prison essay which is discussed in the photojournalism section, I was assisted in the probing of the subject by being able to develop my film while behind the iron fences of the institution. The easy processing enabled me to follow the progress of the story in a positive sense by being able to inspect the pictures taken daily. The processing could have been

1. Unibath is trade name for Cormac Chemical's single solution processing.

done in a closet at the motel, but a changing bag and *Unibath* allowed me to do the work while sitting in a guard's lounge in prison.

The improved film processing techniques for positive and negative color films are also contributing to the creative range of the photographer. Many of the shackles on the creative minds of color photographers are being cut away by the increasing latitude of color emulsions. And with color controls in processing there are opportunities to improve the original image in much the same fashion as black and white photographers have been controlling their pictures for years.

The use of potassium chrome alum is an absolute necessity for high-temperature processing. But it can also serve a more normal use. In the summer time or in climates where hot or warm weather dominates, there is always the danger of reticulation of the film. (Reticulation is the separation of the gelatine of the emulsion with the resulting separation of the image. Small wavy lines occur. Sometimes reticulation looks like grain. In fact, many times grain is blamed when reticulation is the problem.) The use of potassium chrome alum, which is a purple color, aids the film hardening and helps prevent the soft film from damage.

Formula for Potassium Chrome Alum
Potassium Chrome Alum ....1 ounce
Water .... 32 ounces
Dissolve completely and use the solution at or near the same temperature as the developer. Use once and throw away for maximum results.

Film should be hung to dry in dust-free rooms. If possible, there should be no traffic through the areas, as each foot step activates dust particles which could settle on the wet film.

A clean and spotless negative is the greatest time saver in photography. The cleaner the negative, the cleaner will be the print. Even if additional preparation time is required to get the negative ready for printing, the time is well spent if it reduces annoying spotting or work on the print. For example, every negative should be completely dust and lint free before a print is made. If not, literally hundreds of tiny white specks could appear on the print and consume hours of time, spotting them out. If more than one print is needed, you can multiply the problem by the number of prints. Time is saved by cleaning the negative only one time.

What are some of the ways of preparing the film for printing? Assuming the film has been handled properly and needs only the protection from dust, a little film cleaner gently applied to both surfaces with a soft, cotton, lint-free cloth (men's undershirts are good) will wipe the negative clean and place an antistatic coating for continuing the repelling of dust from the negative. The negative will have a temporary protection from dust. An antistatic brush, which is used on the negative as it is placed in the enlarger, will be more effective if the film has the cleaner coating. The applied cleaner will have an effective life of about three weeks and should be used again if the negative is printed after this time.

If a negative has experienced some abuse and shows scratches which print objectionally, you may reduce or eliminate them by the use of corrective chemicals on the negative. A special preparation, which comes bearing several trade names, designed for the correction of scratches is

131. Broken Christ, Louisiana, 1955. The broken figure stuck on the metal cross is given additional importance by highlighting it with Farmer's Reducer on the print.

132. The lone face and eyes are accented by burning-in the other light tones in the composition. By darkening the other tones, the face and eyes take on increased impact.

available. One brand name which is very good is Edwal's *No Scratch*. The application of this chemical on the surface where the scratches appear will reduce noticeably or perhaps eliminate the trouble. If you are in doubt as to which side the *No-Scratch* should be applied, put it on both sides. But, caution should be taken to keep the surfaces free of lint. Any scratch corrective increases the adhesiveness of the surface for foreign particles.

If no chemical especially prepared for scratch correction is available, you may use vaseline. The wax-like salve is rubbed thinly over the surface that contains the scratches. Use your fingers for this, as any cloth will leave some trace of lint. Rub the salve smooth. Place the negative in the enlarger with the greatest care, for anything that touches the surface will probably stick to it. When the printing is finished, clean the film with film cleaner. Do not leave the vaseline on the film.

Scratch correction is not a problem we have to cope with every day, but it does happen and when it occurs you should know the corrective methods to deal with it. Either of the two above mentioned techniques could be used. And they might save some of your most creative work that befell abuse.

After the negative is cleaned and/or treated, it is ready for insertion in the enlarger. If the negative has been cleaned only, use an anti-static brush to wipe the film after it is in the glassless negative carrier. If a glass-type negative carrier is used, brush the negative as it is put into the carrier. *Do not brush* a negative which has been treated for scratches. In fact, do not touch it against any surface after the anti-scratch solution has been applied. If you do, chances are the film will have to be cleaned

and again coated with anti-scratch. It is advisable that each negative be prepared just before printing. Several negatives may be cleaned, if care is taken to keep the cleaned surface from any contact with another surface.

With a clean negative, clean prints will be possible. Periodic cleaning of the enlarger or other printing tools is also a prerequisite to clean prints. A little care in the dark room eliminates remaking of prints, lost time in spotting, and loss of temper.

THE ENLARGEMENT, CONTROLS, AND PROCESSING

While it might be presumptuous, I am going to assume that every reader has at least the basic working knowledge of how to make prints and understands what a good print looks like. Even if you cannot make a top quality print, you can know what it looks like. If you do not feel competent about the making of a print, may I suggest that you get a book on the subject and gain that knowledge before reading this section further. There are several excellent books on print quality.[1] Any of these will prepare you for exploring the creative aspects of the darkroom processes. Our concern is not the act of making a print, but rather the act of using the mechanical processes to a creative advantage. You can only do this if you understand the normal functions of materials and techniques.

[1.] Lootens on Print Quality, J. Ghislain Lootens (Amphoto). Photographic Print Quality, Procedures, and Papers, A. E. Woolley (Chilton). Darkroom techniques, Joseph Foldes, (U.S. Camera).

Tone

A quality print will contain the full range of tones from a rich black to a pure white. Any less tonal range is not an optimum scale print. Since the greater majority of all prints demand optimum scale, you must know how to achieve this quality in a print. But, on occasions, you may have a desire to eliminate tonal latitude in order to strengthen the picture's statement. And if such desire exists, a high contrast print quality might very well contribute creatively to the visual statement. Ofttimes the photographer's reaction or desire to produce the special effect occurs well after the negatives have been shot and processed. The controls possible during shooting and processing are not available. The printing process is the only step that can alter the image. For the high contrast situation, a high contrast paper or filter (for variable contrast papers) is used to reduce or eliminate the grays of the negative and render as near a pure black and white image as possible.

Going to the opposite end of the gray scale, you can often hold down the contrast and retain shadow details which might be lost in normal tonal range prints by using a softer grade contrast paper. For example, a print that contains its optimum tonal scale on a *number two* paper, would exhibit more detail in the darker tones if printed on a *number one* paper. Of course care should be taken not to let the overall contrast go flat or muddy as might happen when the softer grade paper or filter is used. For this kind of control, the variable contrast papers are excellent materials with which to work. The freedom of combining filters and of controlling areas by the use of a filter for that area is an extension of creative control of the image. Single contrast papers are at a disadvantage for this work. Not that single contrast papers will be unworkable, but they are limited in control potential by their singleness of contrast.

High Key and Low Key

The alteration of the tonal scale of a print can be used creatively for the production of high and low-key prints. A high-key print is one that contains almost no gray, only a tiny bit of black, and an abundance of white and gray. A low-key print is one which is predominantly black with a spot of white and almost no light gray. Either of the two effects may be accomplished with middle-key negatives.

A high-key print may be achieved by printing on a high contrast paper which eliminates the middle gray. Or a moderate high contrast paper may be used and the exposure time will be greatly reduced as the print is made. Underprinting will not allow the delicate tones to print. The most transparent areas of the negative will print, producing the black in the print and the lighter tones will be formed by the inadequately printed other shapes and areas. A two-minute print development is a must with this technique and often longer development is desirable. Care should be taken not to get a chemical stain from too-long development. Some papers fog or stain more easily than others, and you should know this before trying an extension of development time.

The dark tones of a low-key print are made possible by using a normal or slightly soft print contrast. The normal paper with a normal middle-key negative will produce excellent low-key results. Printing a

133-134.   Although of the same subject, the top picture is in "low key," the bottom in "high key." Taken at the same time, the difference in the tonal qualities was achieved by moving the camera slightly. The dark tones were made by shooting toward a garage, the lighter tones by shooting toward the snow-covered ground. A Duo-Range 50mm Summicron lens on a Leica M-2 made the close view possible.

second or two longer, or extending the development slightly when the exposure time has been normal, will deepen the dark tones and absorb some of the middle gray creating a rich black which will establish a low latitude of black to white. The highlights or whites will take on added contrast, for they will become more brilliant when compared to the increased quantity of black.

Tonal control of the print is a creative tool. If the photographer is not utilizing this extension to his vision, he is not using all of the devices available for full exploration of his medium. While it is a fact that most photographs will fall into the middle-key, or that special effects will be initiated at the time of exposure, the photographer should *never* be guilty of missing his ob-

jective because of a taboo against darkroom control, or worse, ignorance of the controls possible in the darkroom.

ENLARGING COLOR TRANSPARENCIES TO NEGATIVE PRINTS

The color photographer seldom utilizes the full advantage of his materials with reference to their use in black and white. On many occasions, a dramatic negative print can be made by projecting a color positive transparency as you would use a negative to reverse the positive image into a negative image. The procedure is simple.

Select the transparency which you want to print as a negative effect. Remember that light areas will appear dark and dark areas will appear light on the print. If you

135. The low key of this nude study complements the beauty of the brightly lighted hair. The tones of the picture establish the key of the composition, and the key contributes to the mood.

wish to hold back an area, the process will be the same as with negative-to-positive print making. Or if additional printing or "burning-in" is needed for the darker areas, you would extend the printing time. Other than a complete reversal of tones, the printing or enlarging process will be the same. Perhaps the only precaution will be to keep the image in proper "reading" from left to right. You will have to place the transparency in the enlarger so as to project the image in its proper "left to right" relationship to the original scene.

The printing of color positive transparencies is not a technique which you would use daily, but the results are often dramatic enough that you should be aware of the process.

THE PRINT

How Big?

The decision of how large to make your print is one which only you can decide. Some pictures demand the impact of bigness while other pictures are as strong, even stronger, in a small print size. There is no formula by which you might work to predetermine the size you should make the final print. The only determining factor is the effect the size of the print will have on the viewer. Will the message be seen? With this as your guiding element, every photograph must be measured by its content alone to present effectively the picture in the right dimensions.

In the days of the importance of the salon type exhibitions, the theory was "the bigger the prints, the better the chances of acceptance." One camera club even adapted the philosophy of "big, blue, and

136. The dark, tiny figure is outstanding because of the tones around it.

137A. Ferracyanide was used to lighten the area behind the firefly.

137B. How big should a photograph be? The decision must be made on the basis of subject, the amount of detail wanted, and the distance from which the picture will be viewed. This reproduction is small, but all of the qualities of the picture are evident. Need it be larger?

glossy." The idea of this thinking was that by making a big print, toning it to a hue of blue, and using glossy paper, the photographer would construct a picture of high brilliance and size impact that would demand the judges' attention. The theory was successful for the club's contributors and won acclaim for their prolific exhibition success. But their formula for success is not altogether useful to all photographers. In fact, I do not like the blue toning of black and white prints. On occasion a picture might be made to appear more dramatic in a monochromatic tone other than black, but the picture must fit the color.

The Materials

All non-35mm photographers are awed by the beauty of a big, glossy, sharply detailed 35mm photograph. As a matter of fact, too often the impact of technique allows pictures lacking in creativity to be judged as great photographs. I recommend the use of glossy stock paper. First, there is a cleaner, purer, base white in the paper. The material on which the sensitive emulsion is placed is "white white." This type of base assures you that your print will have a clean white for the highlight areas of the print. Obtaining a full scale of gray is much easier to accomplish with a white base paper than one of the off-white base papers.

If you will examine any book of photographic paper samples, you will find many types of papers with a variety of surfaces. In the description of the paper's characteristics will be found this information: the surface, contrast, base color, and emulsion number. What do these characteristics mean to the creative 35mm photographer?

First, the surface of the paper is all important. Surfaces of papers range from glossy, to silk, to pebble, to suede, to tapestry, to canvas. Most of the surfaces are designed to do specific jobs. The glossy is primarily for reproduction, the silk for portraits or weddings, the canvas for scenics, etc. The photographer makes his choice as the picture content suggests.

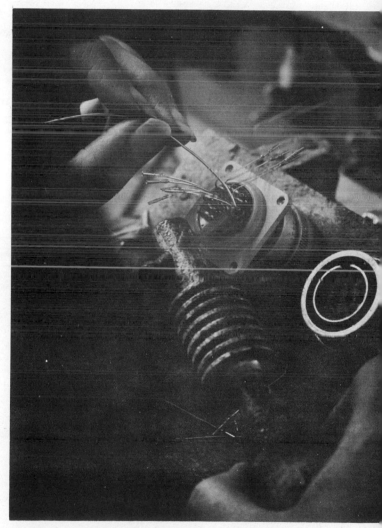

137C. The touch of a soldering operation is accentuated by the delicate tones of the print.

137D. The bathroom fixture is prominent because the darker tones are printed somewhat deeper in color. Printing is subjective and must be used to complete the statement begun in the camera.

137E. The technique of selective focus isolated the water drops on the pine needles.

137F. The texture and design of this picture are strong because of the fidelity of the print-quality tones.

137G. Flashing the top edges of this picture emphasizes the three tots. These seven pictures show a few of the many techniques that may be employed in the printmaking stage to get the most from the negative.

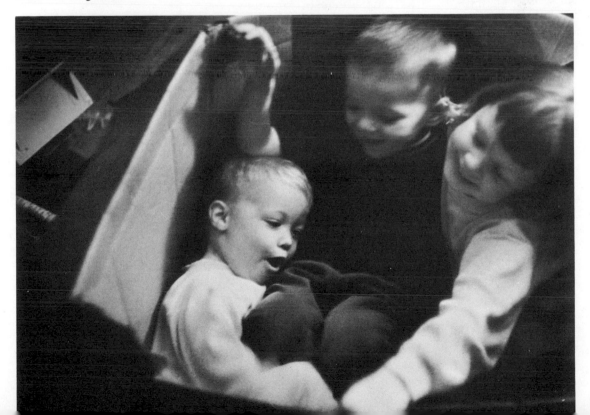

Glossy papers are about the only ones which have a pure white base. Silk surfaces generally have a white, but some contain an off-white color. All other surfaces have some degree of tone departing from the white. When a paper is used that does not contain a white base, the results will be a print that does not have a pure white in the tonal scale. A buff colored paper surface is one which has a dull, light gray base color. The paper is slightly gray before the print exposure is made. When the print exposure is made, the highlights are printed on top of this base buff tone and are reduced from white to an off-white color. If the print is handled properly, the highlight will seldom lose brilliance. The finished print will usually have a slightly yellow tone. For the creative individual, the tonal values of off-white prints could be used effectively for some subjects. But selection and use of the photographic paper should be determined by the functional use of the picture and the visual intent of the photographer.

The contrast of the paper is all important. The matching of the tonal range of the negative to the tonal range of the paper will produce the fullest scale of tones possible. Or, the special effect photograph is achieved by the manipulation of the tonal range of paper and negative. We mentioned this in the high or low-key effect. There are many papers on the market. There are single contrast papers with contrast ranges from #1 or very soft (full gray scale), to #5 or very hard (minimum gray scale). Few negatives will not print on one or more of these contrasts of papers. For quality results or special effects, the single contrast papers may be used.

For the person who wants to minimize his investment in materials, or who wants greater control in a single contrast, the variable contrast papers are recommended. With the filters designed for the variable papers, the photographer has an unusually wide range of controls. The creative print maker can exert maximum control over his photograph. Variations in tone, depth of color, and mixing of filters are possible.

The emulsion number in black and white photography is not as critical as in color photography. But it might be well to know that at times a paper will vary in reaction to light or tone from emulsion to emulsion. For this reason, when matched prints are to be made in quantity, they should be made from the same emulsion number. For single prints or small print groups, the importance of the emulsion number for continuity is of little significance. The reason the emulsion number is important to the creative print maker is that the making of a print from one batch of paper will often produce a different tonal value from a print from the same negative printed on another emulsion number.

On Cropping

In the techniques on shooting and composition we discussed the merits and demerits of altering the negative. The photographer has the opportunity to second-guess his picture as he makes the print, if he chooses to do so. Most creative 35mm users place such demands on themselves at the moment of exposure that print cropping is not even considered. But times arise when cropping is desirable and necessary. The negative should never be cropped without careful consideration to the reconstructed composition. Be sure the redesigned composition is stronger than the original. An excellent test for you to undertake in searching out the value of cropping a picture is to take a negative and make as many prints as possible with the strongest designs. Display these so that you and other people may view them for a few days. Then discuss the pictures for their effect on the viewers. Be sure that among the pictures displayed is a full print.

Try to make the cropped pictures seem printed from different negatives. Compare the cropped prints to the original. If the original composition holds up in the evaluation, you know that your eye for instantaneous selection of elements of compositions is strong and re-evaluation in the darkroom will be less and less needed. Special projects can be greatly improved by judicious or radical cropping of the original picture. Cropping is a creative technique not to be overlooked when the picture is improved by its use.

Grain

The strength of grain in a print may be increased further in the printing procedure by using a higher contrast paper than normal. Conversely, grain may be lessened or softened by using a softer contrast in the print. A negative that has been overexposed or overdeveloped will have a tendency toward increased grain. If the desire to accentuate this grain exists, you should use at least two contrasts higher paper in making the print. For example, if the negative is either overdeveloped or overexposed, but still in the normal or number two range of paper contrast, you can accentuate the grain by using a number four contrast paper. The grain will appear sharper because of the increase in

138. Cajun country, Louisiana,1955. A composition created in the camera should be so closely united that no alteration can be made in the printing. This picture cannot be cropped without affecting the design and balance.

contrast. Likewise, if the grain is disturbing, the negative could be printed on a number one paper and by reducing the contrast, the sharpness of the grain would be reduced. Grain too, is an element of photography over which the creative 35mm photographer has considerable control. Employing the use of grain for special effects can produce exciting photographs.

TONE AS AN ELEMENT OF DESIGN

Too often, photographers think of the tonal scale as a mechanical operation. Tone can be a creative element of design that begins with the original scene, is transmitted to the film, processed, and then presented in the print. The strength of the tonal range of the print has a great influ-

139. Sharon, Connecticut, 1961. A single-lens reflex with a flip mirror permits composition at the time of shooting, eliminating uncertainty as to the picture's content in the print.

140. Printing photographs that have both indoor and outdoor lighting presents a problem in exposure control. The interior and the exterior must have equal quality. Most often, multi-contrast type papers are used for this kind of control. Varigam was used for this print.

141. Ben Karp, sculptor, 1959. Maximum print tone control is achieved with filters and Varigam paper.

142. A. Sidney Poitier, 1957.
B. Art Opening, Sharon, Connecticut, 1961.
C. Dutchess College, Poughkeepsie, New York, 1961.

These three pictures are examples of the maximum range of tones that is possible. The success of each picture depends on the retention of all the tonal values of the original scene.

A.

B.

C.

143. Even on days when the weather is terrible, pictures with full tonal scale may be made by using printing techniques on the negative. There was a steady rain falling at the time this picture was taken and the light was very low and gray. Contrast was added in the print.

144. Claude Monteux and Mrs. Vincent Astor, Rhinebeck, New York, 1961. Don't be afraid to print pictures that show excessive grain. Many times, the extra texture of the grain pattern will pull an ordinary picture up to a dramatic one.

145. There are times when the very nature and strength of the picture depends on the tones of the print. Taken with a Leica 90mm Elmar lens and Pus X film, this shot of flowers within the shadow of the photographer depends on the contrast of the light against the dark.

146. Cat, French Quarter, New Orleans, Louisiana, 1953. The range of tonal scale from the cat in the shadow to the highlights in the balcony had to be maintained to make this print successful.

147. $56,000 Pony, 1957. Flashing the sky section accents the figures of the pony and the man. (Taken for *Look Magazine*.)

ence over the success of the picture. I am not referring to contrast or key at this point. I am making reference to the relationship of tones. When is white, white? How black is black? Can a middle gray print have contrast? These are the basic questions asked when tone is considered as design.

When is white, white? I once had an art teacher who illustrated the relative theory of color as pertaining to contrast of tones by answering the question of when white is white. He would show that white is white only when seen in relationship to a darker tone. To test this he suggested that a handprint be placed on a white refrigerator door. The hand mark adds separation to the tones and the white appears more brilliant.

How black is black? The same theory is true for the dark tones. The richness of black only becomes evident when a lighter tone of smaller size is placed adjacent to it. For your own satisfaction, take a piece of black paper and place a tiny white object on it. The black will deepen and the white will stand out. Some colors will be more dominant than others. For example, the brighter colors such as red will be seen first. If you are working with color materials, color dominance is very important. Bright colors have a feeling of coming forward or moving faster than the subtle colors of blue or green.

An interesting case in court involving an art professor adds strength to this theory. Dr. Kenneth Winebrenner of Buffalo, New York, was given a ticket for speeding. He was driving a red sports car. The radar did not indicate which of the several cars in the four-lane highway was to be stopped. The policeman selected Dr. Winebrenner's car. In court Dr. Winebren-ner pleaded his case as one of man's reaction to bright color. He contended the traffic officer had only reacted as normal reaction to color would dictate. His red car was more easily seen than the other blue, gray, or tan cars that surrounded him. He won his case.

In black and white tones you react to the relationship of black to white to gray. The lighter tones are seen with more ease and register stronger impressions. When the lighter tones are seen in contrast to darker tones, the fullest strength of tonality is accomplished. When white is placed in contrast to white, the black commands attention. When can a gray print have contrast? By this theory of the dominance of the tone of the major area when contrasted to the tone of the minor area, gray can be made to appear strong by having a small amount of black in the composition. The black can be added in the print by overprinting or flashing the print (See page 33, *Photographic Print Quality*, A.E. Woolley, Chilton Publisher for the description of the technique of flashing). The view of the pony and boy is given stronger tonal values by the darker tone of the sky. These areas were flashed on the print.

Tone in photography is the application of relative values of the gray scale. The tonal strength of a print is measured by the effectiveness of the comparison of the relationship.

IN SUMMARY . . .

The many useful and creative techniques of the thirty-five millimeter camera, lenses, and accessories have been defined, discussed, and illustrated. But there are still many devices of design and creative

148. Kingston, New York, 1961. Strong blacks are necessary to the composition of this picture.

149. Adlai Stevenson, Hyde Park, New York, 1961. A 200mm lens focused on Mr. Stevenson isolates him from the TV camera in the foreground. The print was made to keynote the light tones of his face.

150. Woodstock, New York, 1958. The camera set at hyperfocal for f:11 was used to make this photograph. The gray scale from the shadow to the highlight was controlled in the printing.

151. Thaddeus Okatch, Kenya, Africa, 1961. Close cropping at the time of shooting emphasized the cat. Control in the printing stage regulates the variation of tone.

imagery which remain for discovery and use. The words and pictures in this book are intended to make you think, to stimulate, to motivate, and even to make you angry if it takes that to stimulate you to take up camera and make pictures. No one can stand over your shoulder and say, "Now press the shutter release." A teacher can only inform the student of working principles and techniques. He cannot do the work for the student. A book can only serve the same role as the teacher. The desire to make use of the material one reads remains the action of the photographer.

Photography, and especially the area of thirty-five millimeter photography, is only an infant in the world of creative fields. The medium to date has had only surface exploration. As mechanical, chemical, and technical improvements broaden the range of physical adaptations of the camera to creative terms, photography will achieve greater meaning. No longer is photography an imitator of approved art techniques. Photography is an art technique unique in itself. No longer must photographers apologize for the medium in which they work. Often they are envied by the other artists, because of the greater flexibility of the photographic processes. The debate on whether photography is an art is useless talk now. The important thing is learning, applying, and exploring the elements and techniques that make photography a creative medium. Every photographer can make a contribution to these greater horizons.

INDEX